Gluten-Free
Dairy-Free
COOKBOOK

Gluten-Free Dairy-Free

COOKBOOK

100 Satisfying, Family-Friendly Recipes

DANIELLE FAHRENKRUG

Photography by Hélène Dujardin

ROCKRIDGE
PRESS

Interior and Cover Designer: Lisa Schreiber

Art Producer: Meg Baggott

Editor: Daniel Edward Petrino

Production Editor: Emily Sheehan

Photography © 2020 Hélène Dujardin.

Food styling by Anna Hampton.

ISBN: Print 978-1-64611-498-6 | eBook 978-1-64611-499-3

R0

This book is dedicated to each
of you who are reading this,
that you may always thrive
and be nourished.

Contents

Introduction

ALL AROUND THE WORLD, the gluten-free dairy-free diet is becoming a popular lifestyle. A large part of this is because many people are being diagnosed with celiac disease, while others have various forms of gluten and/or dairy sensitivities. Ultimately a dairy-free and gluten-free lifestyle provides success with healing, overall well-being, and a more nourishing diet, and helps turn many health problems into a thing of the past.

When I first transitioned into a gluten-free diet it was due to my own choice, for health reasons. At the ripe age of 26 I found out I had PCOS (polycystic ovarian syndrome) and was already monitoring a form of hemochromatosis (a blood disorder). I clearly remember the day I was sitting at the doctor's office with my fiancé just months before our wedding and hearing the words, "You may not be able to have children due to these cysts." That struck a chord with me, and at that moment I set out on a mission to "cure" myself. After tons of research and questions, I had a whole new outlook and understanding of the relationship between food and health. I started by changing my diet and detoxing from gluten. I continued to research and learn everything there was to know about gluten and dairy, and processed foods and how they can alter hormones, cause leaky gut and depression, affect brain clarity, and prevent proper nutrient absorption. This was also contributing to my blood disorder. Once I started focusing on a diet of real, whole foods and eliminating gluten, dairy, and processed foods, everything changed and we were able to conceive completely naturally. We now have two incredible and healthy boys! My extremely high iron levels decreased (with continous monitoring), and my cholesterol balanced out. During this time of finding balance and healing, I was eating more food than before, felt full of radiant energy, and looked better than I had in years!

I remember the hoaxes and rumors about this way of clean eating, the panic of missing out on our favorite foods, and the worry that it would be time-consuming and expensive. None of which is true. I have been able to eat amazing foods without the guilt or dreaded bloat, and I have the recipes to prove it! I want to help you understand that when you eat healthier, nutrient-dense foods and eliminate gluten and dairy, you'll start to heal from the inside out. You'll notice better overall health, clearer skin, and more energy. Through my experience, by maximizing your absorption of the necessary vitamins and minerals the body needs, you'll also reduce salt, sugar, and fat cravings because your body will feel fueled and satisfied!

Going gluten-free and dairy-free isn't just about what you can't eat. There are tons of wonderful foods to enjoy, and this is your guide to making everyday dishes delectable, healthy, and fun for everyone! Whether you are new to gluten-free dairy-free eating or just living with someone who has an intolerance, discover the wonderful foods you can still enjoy.

This book doesn't rely on extra salt, sugar, or nondairy butter, yogurt, and sour cream for flavor. I have a way around that and you will see that there are plenty of ways to get those cheesy, tangy, and creamy flavors that we so often crave. This is your new guide to freedom with food!

CHAPTER 1

The Gluten-Free Dairy-Free Kitchen

I COMPLETELY UNDERSTAND that going gluten-free AND dairy-free may seem overwhelming and it may leave you feeling a little deprived at first. But rest assured, there are all kinds of wonderful foods to enjoy, and the recipes in this book will show you how. I am here to walk you through every step of the way as you transition to this new way of eating.

As you embrace your gluten-free dairy-free lifestyle, properly converting your kitchen is the first step and a major key to transitioning your food environment. To start: Wash out all cabinets, drawers, pantries, and the refrigerator (with nontoxic cleaner) to get rid of all gluten particles and to prevent contamination as you introduce new foods. Some appliances and tools (such as cutting boards and wooden spoons) should ideally be replaced.

The next step is to return all your gluten-free dairy-free items to your cupboards, being sure to double-check that all dressings, condiments, dips, and canned or boxed items have no gluten or dairy ingredients. You may be surprised at how many of these everyday items contain gluten and/or dairy.

When it comes to restocking your kitchen, some staple items to get you started are gluten-free pasta, a gluten-free bread loaf, corn tortillas, rice, quinoa, psyllium husk, flaxseed meal, and nutritional yeast. Nutritional yeast is wonderful to have on hand for adding to creamy dishes and to give a "cheese" flavor. Keep canned coconut milk on hand to make creamy soups, sauces, and sweet treats. Stock up on gluten-free flours, too. Start with a basic gluten-free flour mix (make sure it is dairy-free, too) so you are not overwhelmed with additional flours. Then, gradually include tapioca flour, quinoa flour, potato starch, cornstarch, and xanthan gum. Keep certified gluten-free rolled oats and gluten-free quick-cooking oats around for breakfasts and to turn into oat flour by grinding in a food processor when needed. (Or purchase gluten-free oat flour.) My kids love eating oats for breakfast with coconut sugar, cinnamon, and a splash of nondairy milk or peanut butter. A family favorite recipe is Peanut Butter and Chocolate Swirl Overnight Oats (page 28), so we always have oats around!

The Benefits of Eating Gluten-Free Dairy-Free

One in 100 people worldwide is diagnosed with celiac disease. Common symptoms include digestive issues, cramping, bloating, depression, anxiety, anemia, infertility, skin disorders, brain fog, irritability, weight loss, vomiting, diarrhea, constipation, and, in children especially, ADHD, neurological disorders, failure to thrive, poor growth, and malnutrition. Celiac disease is an autoimmune disorder that attacks the villi, the small protrusions in the intestines responsible for absorbing vital nutrients. The damage can lead to leaky gut syndrome and is responsible for the discomfort you may be feeling. Some people with a mild case, known as nonceliac gluten sensitivity (NCGS), may experience the same symptoms, just not as extreme as a person with celiac disease. Gluten sensitivity and celiac disease are also commonly linked with lactose intolerance. This breakdown of the intestinal lining also prevents the body from properly digesting the sugars found in dairy, and because the gut is already damaged, dairy can produce the same uncomfortable symptoms as gluten.

The good news is your body can heal itself with the right nutrition, especially through easy, healthy recipes. By eliminating gluten and dairy, the gut is given a chance to repair. In some cases, dairy and gluten may be slowly reintroduced into your diet. But trust me, once you start feeling clean and lean and extraordinary without it, you may never want gluten and dairy back in your life.

The benefits of eating gluten-free and dairy-free are remarkable:

INCREASED VIBRANT ENERGY. As your body and intestines are healed, they're able to absorb the proper nutrients they need, increasing energy.

DECREASED BLOATING, DIARRHEA, AND CONSTIPATION. Eliminating gluten and dairy prevents the lining of the intestines from being attacked by the gluten protein. This attack occurs during digestion and typically causes pain, discomfort, constipation, bloating, and diarrhea.

NO MORE MUSCLE CRAMPING OR NAUSEA. Cramping can occur due to lack of potassium and water. Celiac and NCGS patients often experience diarrhea or vomiting when gluten is consumed, which can lead to dehydration. Avoiding gluten consumption can prevent vomiting and allows the body to remain hydrated. Make sure to drink plenty of water every day as your body heals.

HAPPIER WITH DECREASED ANXIETY AND DEPRESSION. You may find anxiety and depression subsiding as your body is able to properly absorb endorphin-stimulating vitamins such as B_{12} and folate.

CLEARER THINKING. You may have heard your gut is your second brain. Your brain can't function optimally if there is damage to the stomach lining from gluten and/or dairy products. This damage prevents the proper absorption of essential vitamins, minerals, carbohydrates, protein, lipids, and other essential nutrients that help our brain function at its peak. It can also cause inflammation, which may cause depression, anxiety, and brain fog.

Common and Hidden Sources of Dairy

Reading food labels is essential to spotting the hidden dairy that manufacturers put into foods. Dairy adds texture and bounce to baked goods, richness to egg dishes, and creaminess to sauces, dips, and dressings. Dried milk, which is often added to foods such as protein bars, crackers, cookies, soups, quiche, and condiments, can contain gluten, so check the label, even if the product says gluten-free on the packaging. The uplifting news is that there is a plethora of nondairy sources that taste just as delicious, are lower in saturated fat, cholesterol, and calories, and are overall much healthier choices.

I always keep nondairy milk, coconut oil, and plant-based butter around for baking and cooking. Almond milk is one of my favorites for making lattes and smoothies. I love to use cashew milk and canned coconut milk for creamy curries and soups. These gluten- and dairy-free alternatives are used throughout this book and allow you to enjoy foods like comforting chocolate fudge pops, thick cheesecake, and creamy macaroni and cheese without the guilt, dairy, or gluten.

Nondairy Milk Alternatives

Dairy is typically used to add flavor, texture, and moisture to recipes. With the array of nondairy milk alternatives available today, it's easy to re-create your favorite delicious dishes without using dairy products. Many dairy-free alternatives to milk, yogurt, cheese, spreads, ice creams, and whipped toppings are rich in plant nutrients, omega-3 fatty acids, and protein. Keeping these dairy-free alternatives on hand is essential for adding moisture and creaminess to recipes as you start cooking dairy- and gluten-free.

Each nondairy milk has its own texture and flavor, so be sure to try out a few varieties to determine what suits your tastes. I love to use cashew for its creamy texture. Different milks work well in different recipes. For example, rice, almond, and soy milk are more watery than hemp, oat, and cashew milk, so they work better in baked goods rather than creamy sauces. Nondairy milk can be substituted wherever dairy milk is called for in a recipe. Choose unsweetened or original-flavor varieties for baking and savory dishes.

The following is a list of nondairy milks and ways I use them.

ALMOND

Almond milk is made by soaking almonds in water, crushing and blending them, and then straining the liquid. It comes in vanilla or original flavors, and some brands include added sugars. For baking I suggest using original flavor without sugar. This milk is delicious and works well in smoothies, oatmeal, and baked goods such as muffins and pancakes.

CASHEW

Cashew milk is made by soaking raw cashews in water, crushing and blending them, and then straining the liquid. It is thicker than other nondairy milks and has a slightly sweet taste. Use cashew milk for dressings, soups, and smoothies.

COCONUT

Coconut milk comes in various forms including coconut milk beverage, canned full-fat coconut milk, canned lite coconut milk, and canned coconut cream. Canned coconut milk is close to the creaminess of whole dairy milk or cream.

NUTRITIONAL YEAST

Nutritional yeast adds a delectable punch of cheesy, Parmesan-like flavor to dishes, without the dairy. Nutritional yeast comes from a species of yeast known as *Saccharomyces cerevisiae*. It's different from baker's yeast, which is the form of yeast that helps bread rise. Nutritional yeast goes through a heating and drying process that causes it to be inactive. Since it's not an animal product and doesn't contain nuts, it's a great addition for anyone with food allergies. Nutritional yeast is incredibly nutritious and rich in B vitamins, potassium, calcium, protein, and iron. It boosts energy, helps the immune system, promotes healthy skin, nails, and hair, and more. Add it to vegan cheese spreads, sauces, soups, and macaroni and cheese, or sprinkle it over popcorn. You can find nutritional yeast at most grocery stores in the bulk section or natural foods area or online. Store it in a cool, dry, dark place for up to two years.

It's made from shredded coconut flesh combined with water that is then strained into a creamy, rich, and slightly sweet liquid. Coconut milk separates when canned and should be shaken before using. The low-fat (lite) variety has more separation than the full-fat or cream as it contains more water and less cream. Canned coconut cream works well for homemade whipped cream or as a substitute for dairy cream.

HEMP

Hemp milk is made by soaking hemp seeds in water, blending the mixture, and then straining the liquid. Hemp has an earthy flavor and a texture similar to cow's milk. Use in smoothies, dressings, and baked goods, and over granola or oats.

OAT

Oat milk is made by soaking oats in water, blending the mixture, and then straining the liquid. Oat milk is very creamy and delicious with a hint of oaty flavor. It works well as a substitute for dairy in baking and oatmeal.

RICE

Like the other milks, rice milk is formed by straining soaked and blended rice. The consistency is much thinner than nut, oat, or hemp milk. Rice milk is very light in texture and flavor. It works well as a milk substitute in recipes like pancakes.

SOY

Soybeans that have been soaked in water, blended, and strained form soy milk. It's creamy and delicious and a great alternative when a recipe calls for nondairy milk.

Other Dairy Concerns and Substitutes

Cooking dairy-free comes with a set of concerns all its own, such as what are the proper substitutions to make without skimping on flavor? Nowadays we're fortunate enough to have many dairy-free items available in stores, but finding substitutes that work properly can be tricky. After all, the main ingredients in creamy mac and cheese are cheese and butter. Swapping coconut oil for butter results in an unsatisfying dish. Throughout this book I share my beloved recipes for dairy-free milks, chocolate, butters, and cheeses that keep food tasting so good you never miss the dairy! This book provides plenty of cheesy, tangy, creamy flavors to satisfy your cravings.

CHOCOLATE

Pure chocolate is a dairy-free food, but manufacturers often add things like milk solids, milk powders, butterfat, or cream to milk chocolate. These dairy products may contaminate many brands of semisweet and dark chocolate if they're processed in the same factory. You can contact the manufacturer to see if they cross-contaminate during processing, or use a brand that is made exclusively for those with allergen sensitivities. In our home I like to use Enjoy Life brand, especially their semisweet chocolate chips, mini chocolate chips, and chocolate chunks. This allergen-free chocolate can be found online and in almost all grocery stores. When purchasing cocoa powder, make sure to reach for pure cocoa powder with no added dairy ingredients.

CLARIFIED BUTTER AND GHEE

Is clarified butter or ghee okay to consume on a dairy-free diet? The answer is that it may not cause problems for lactose-intolerant people and may even be safe for those with milk allergies. During the process of heating the butter, the milk solids, casein, and water are removed and all that remains is butterfat. Butterfat does contain dairy but is lactose-free since the milk solids are removed. However, there is no guarantee that there won't be traces of casein or whey, which is why I do not use clarified butter or ghee in this book.

CHEESE

There are many store-bought alternatives to dairy cheese. But don't run out and buy one of every variety. Dairy-free cheese does have a different taste from dairy cheese, so it's best to gradually transition. I suggest eliminating cheese completely to allow for the cheese cravings to subside. This way, as you incorporate dairy-free cheese into your diet, the texture and satisfaction you once enjoyed will be restored. Some dairy-free cheeses are made from nuts and others from plant-based sources such as pea protein. You can find sliced and shredded cheese in mozzarella and Cheddar flavors at most grocery stores in the vegan or cheese section. These work nicely in pasta dishes, lasagna, quesadillas, and pizza. I make a nut-based queso at home, and in this book I'll show you how to make nut-based Vegan Ricotta Cheese (page 166). Trader Joe's has a lovely almond-based shredded cheese that I love. It does not melt well but has a cheese flavor that is not as "fake" as other nondairy cheeses, although it does contain 1 percent lactose, so make sure to read labels carefully. Other brands such as So Delicious, Miyoko's, Violife, and Daiya have a slightly different flavor than regular cheese and melt very well for cheese sauces. Just be sure to read labels, as some vegan cheeses are made from barley, which contains gluten.

Dairy Alternative Substitution Chart

Throughout these recipes you will find that you may not have certain ingredients on hand. For example, if you are making a pie and it calls for canned coconut milk and all you have are cashew and oat milk, which one is best to use? This guide will help make swapping out ingredients easy while producing winning results.

ALMOND MILK (1 CUP)

1 cup canned lite coconut milk

OR

1 cup boxed coconut milk beverage

OR

1 cup cashew milk

OR

1 cup soy milk

CASHEW MILK, HOMEMADE

Substitute pecans or almonds for the cashews

COCONUT MILK, FULL-FAT (1 CUP)

1 cup cashew milk (although it will be thinner)

OR

1 cup canned coconut cream

OAT MILK (1 CUP)

1 cup hemp milk

OR

1 cup cashew milk

CHEESE, SHREDDED

Use equal amounts of a favorite brand, such as Trader Joe's, Miyoko's, Daiya, Violife, or So Delicious. Any cheese can be used, but please note that almond-based cheeses don't melt as well as others. For creamy sauces it is best to use Daiya and So Delicious brands.

COCONUT CREAM

If using it in pies and soups, you can substitute canned full-fat coconut milk. When using coconut cream for a whipped topping, you can substitute an equal amount of aquafaba.

COCONUT OIL

This can be swapped out for equal parts vegan butter. Vegan butter comes as a spread or in stick form like regular butter. To avoid a coconut taste when sautéing, use refined (rather than virgin) coconut oil.

NONDAIRY YOGURT

In baking only, equal amounts of unsweetened applesauce

OR

Equal amounts of unsweetened pumpkin puree, but this will alter the flavor

Common and Hidden Sources of Gluten

Gluten is a protein found in all sorts of grains: wheat, barley, rye, and oats (unless they are labeled as certified gluten-free). A gluten-free diet aims to eliminate all the gluten from those grains and foods derived from them. This means bread, pasta, and pastries have to be made with gluten-free flour.

Gluten lurks in everyday foods and products, such as sauces, salad dressings, frozen treats, soups, bread, cookies, candy, pasta, crackers, and other baked goods. Replace them with eggs, fruit, and veggies for breakfast; rice, corn, or potatoes for lunch; and salad with oil and vinegar for dinner. Even medicine, toothpaste, chewing gum, makeup, soaps, and shampoos may contain gluten. Once it's in your system, it will cause the same degree of chaos as if you had haphazardly eaten a donut. Eating out requires special caution, as the restaurant's toaster, fryer, and utensils may allow for cross-contamination. If you have any doubts about store-bought gluten-free foods, connect with the manufacturer for confirmation the product is 100 percent gluten-free.

Now you may be wondering why gluten is in so many products and foods and what the hype is all about. Gluten was originally used in the early twentieth century as a food stabilizer, giving treats such as ice creams the density needed to prevent melting when handled. Back then, gluten was neither widespread nor refined to the point of causing health problems the same way it commonly does today. One major concern today is that the US Food and Drug Administration (FDA) considers labeling food "gluten-free" to be voluntary by manufacturers.

You can easily avoid gluten-laden foods and products by reading labels carefully and diving into the world of mouthwatering gluten-free natural foods, such as chickpea, quinoa, and gluten-free oats. Always look for the "certified gluten-free" logo, which ensures the product hasn't been processed using the same machinery used for wheat products. Consider gluten sensitivity as an opportunity to explore the rich tastes of foods you've never heard of before.

Gluten-Free Flours and Starches

There are numerous gluten-free flours and starches to choose from, but not all of them are created equal. Understanding the proper methods for mixing them is key for creating successful dishes.

First, it is important to know what these flours are. Unlike wheat flours, gluten-free flours are made from whole and ancient grains that contain no gluten. In baking, these gluten-free flours need leavening and binding agents to work properly. To create these gluten-free flours, grains such as teff, amaranth, sorghum, buckwheat, rice, certified gluten-free oats, corn, and quinoa are ground into a fine powder. Nuts and produce such as almonds, dried banana, and coconut are also used to make gluten-free flours. The good news is these flours are plant-based and hold more nutritional value than processed white flours (which have had their nutrients stripped away and are then fortified to add them back in).

Gluten-free starches are derived from root vegetables. Root vegetables are well tolerated by people with gluten intolerance. Starches include arrowroot starch, tapioca starch/flour, and potato starch. These starches act as natural thickening agents in place of flour. They are used to thicken soups and stews, pie fillings, and sauces, and to make gluten-free baking powder.

Some flours are too dense to stand on their own, and others are too light. Dense flours work best when blended with lighter flours and/or starches, additional leavening, and extra liquid. Lighter flours absorb moisture quickly; on their own they produce flat baked goods with too much moisture. For example, tapioca flour, potato starch, and cornstarch are all very light and work best blended with dense flours such as rice, almond meal, buckwheat, and coconut flour. Finding the appropriate combination and knowing how these flours work together unlocks the magic to gluten-free cooking success.

Luckily, to make this simple as you move through this process, gluten-free flour blends are readily available in stores. In my experience, the various brands can be quite different and may result in baked goods that are either too dry or too moist. When not using my own gluten-free flour blend (which is in my first cookbook, *Dairy-Free Gluten-Free Baking Cookbook*), I like to use Bob's Red Mill Gluten-Free 1 to 1 Baking Flour and Krusteaz Gluten Free All Purpose Flour, both of which were tested in these recipes.

Our world is full of choices, and the last thing you need to worry about is stocking your pantry with 20 different flours. Since flour options can be overwhelming, the recipes in this book use only a few of these flours in an effort to make the recipes easier on your budget. To save money, purchase these flours in the bulk section of your grocery store if available. Below is your guide to understanding many of the flours available today.

ALMOND FLOUR

Almond flour or meal is made from finely ground almonds and imparts a sweet flavor to baked goods. It is great for cakes and muffins as it holds moisture well and is a good substitute for wheat. It may need an extra binding agent, such as egg or tapioca starch, in baking applications. It is high in protein, fiber, and healthy fats. Go for "blanched" almond meal or flour, which has no skins and a more neutral taste in baked goods and cookies. Store in an airtight container in a cool, dry place. Almond flour can be found in most grocery stores and in the bulk section of specialty grocery stores.

ALL-PURPOSE GLUTEN-FREE FLOUR

Companies started making gluten-free flour blends for convenience, but some contain dairy to make baked goods light and fluffy, or nuts for extra buoyancy and moisture. When using an all-purpose gluten-free flour blend, make sure to check the label to ensure it doesn't contain dairy or milk powders. If you have a nut allergy, make sure to check all labels for that as well. My favorite brands are Bob's Red Mill and Krusteaz.

BROWN RICE, WHITE RICE, AND SWEET WHITE RICE FLOUR

Rice flour is the most common gluten-free flour and is used in most store-bought mixes. It comes from three sources: brown rice, white rice, and high-starch short-grain sweet rice (glutinous rice). The flours are made by grinding the grains into powders. Sweet white rice flour is sweeter due to its high carbohydrate content and is ideal for baked goods, thickening sauces, and making rice noodles and mochi. Rice flour in general is a heavy flour, and more water may be required when using it in baking. It mixes best with other gluten-free flours and light starches. Store in an airtight container or jar in a cool, dry place. Look for rice flours in the baking section or bulk section of grocery stores.

BUCKWHEAT FLOUR

Buckwheat is the fruit of a plant that is dried and ground into a flour. It is not a type of wheat, despite the name. It has a strong, robust flavor and is high in protein, fiber, and B vitamins. It is very dense and heavy and works well when mixed with light starches. It can be found online or in most specialty stores.

COCONUT FLOUR

Coconut flour is great for baked goods as it adds natural sweetness. It is nutritious, low carb, and packed with fiber. It does not substitute for wheat, as it is a denser flour, and mixtures that use it may need more liquid or less flour for baking. Coconut flour works well in baked goods when combined with almond flour, which adds moisture and bounce. Store in an airtight container or jar in a cool, dry place. Coconut flour can be found in most grocery stores in the baking section.

OAT FLOUR

Oats can be ground into a fine powder that is high in fiber, protein, and iron. They add wonderful structure and fiber to cookies, muffins, quick breads, and pancakes. Make sure the oats are labeled certified gluten-free as some are cross-contaminated with wheat when they are grown side by side. Oats soak up loads of moisture, so when used in baking, extra liquid and settling time after mixing with other ingredients may be necessary. In baked goods, oats blend well with lighter flours as they help bind the ingredients. Store in an airtight container or jar in a cool, dry place. Look for oat flour in the baking section, breakfast section, or bulk section of grocery stores.

POTATO STARCH

Potato starch is derived from potatoes and is a light and very fine powder. (Potato flour is different: It is made from ground-up dehydrated potatoes.) It adds structure to gluten-free baking, lending a soft, chewy consistency to homemade breads, pizza crust, and baked goods. Potato starch works best when mixed with other gluten-free flours, as it cannot hold its own in baked goods. If avoiding nightshade vegetables, you can use cornstarch in place of potato starch. Store in an airtight container or jar in a cool, dry place. Potato starch can be found in most grocery stores in the baking section or bulk section.

QUINOA FLOUR

Quinoa flour is an incredibly nutrient-rich and moist gluten-free flour milled from a grain native to the Andes Mountains in South America. It is rich in B vitamins, amino acids, and fiber. Quinoa flour has a nutty flavor that can overpower baked goods. It is best when mixed with other gluten-free flours or used to bind meat patties such as hamburgers or veggie burgers. It can be found online and in most specialty stores.

SORGHUM FLOUR

Sorghum flour, also known as milo and jowar, is available in red and white varieties. It has a slightly sweet flavor and is high in fiber and protein. It is dense and works best in baking when combined with other gluten-free flours. Sorghum is often used in packaged gluten-free flour blends mixed with tapioca flour, potato starch, and both brown and white rice flours. Store in an airtight container or jar in a cool, dry place. Look for sorghum flour in most specialty grocery stores or online.

TAPIOCA STARCH

Tapioca starch or flour is made from the cassava plant. It is a light powder that mixes well with heavy gluten-free flours such as rice, buckwheat, or coconut flour. It naturally helps bind foods, helping baked goods hold their shape. With a slightly sweet flavor, it's good for thickening soups and sauces. Too much tapioca flour can cause baked goods and sauces to have a chewy or rubbery texture since it also acts as a binding agent. Store in an airtight container or jar in a cool, dry place. Tapioca starch can be found in most grocery stores in the baking section or bulk section.

TEFF FLOUR

Teff flour is a staple in Ethiopia and is available in North America in dark and light varieties. It aids circulation and weight loss and is packed with calcium, phosphorus (helps balance hormones naturally), fiber, and protein. With a mildly nutty flavor, it works well in pancakes, waffles, and quick breads when combined with other gluten-free flours. Store in an airtight container or jar in a cool, dry place. It can be hard to find; look for it in specialty grocery stores or online.

CHICKPEA FLOUR

Chickpea flour, also known as besan, gram, or garbanzo bean flour, is made from ground chickpeas. It is naturally gluten-free and rich in protein, fiber, and other vitamins and minerals. Chickpea flour works well in baking when combined with other gluten-free flours. It is nutty and dense and adds complexity to baked goods. It works well when combined with a light starch such as potato or tapioca. Alone, it works well as a binder in veggie burgers and fritters. It also makes delicious thin pancakes such as crepes. Store in an airtight container or jar in a cool, dry place. You can find it in most grocery stores in the baking section and in the bulk section.

Other Key Ingredients

Binders are an essential element in gluten-free baking. Since gluten is the "glue" that holds traditional baked goods together, it must be replaced. Think about that favorite fluffy baked muffin you cherish. It needs a binding agent to hold its shape and keep it from falling apart on your lap with every bite. Popular binding agents in baked goods include eggs, flaxseed, psyllium husk, chia seeds, guar gum, xanthan gum, and, in some cases, pumpkin or banana puree.

Store all of these items in a sealed container in a cool, dark, dry place like the pantry.

BAKING SODA AND BAKING POWDER

Two ingredients that help leaven foods are baking soda and baking powder. Both provide fluffiness to muffins and breads when yeast is not involved. Each can have an impact on the results of your baked goods. Too much baking soda can cause a bitter taste, and too little can cause foods not to rise properly, which is where the addition of baking powder is needed. Using the correct proportions helps you achieve high-quality cookies, cakes, flatbreads, and more.

Baking soda (sodium bicarbonate) is an alkaline leavening agent. Picture grade school and experimenting with baking soda mixed with vinegar. When the two are mixed, you get major fizzy bubbling action overflowing from cups or out of volcanoes.

Baking powder is a powdered leavening agent for baked goods made of three components: an alkali, an acid, and a filler. It's a mixture of baking soda (alkali), cream of tartar (acid), and a filler such as cornstarch or arrowroot starch (for grain-free). Most commonly it's used in recipes that are alkaline instead of acidic (meaning recipes that also use lemon, lime, or vinegar in the ingredients). Baking powder works well in foods that do not use yeast and expands the batter slowly for quick breads, pancakes, waffles, cakes, soda bread, and other baked goods. It doesn't impart a bitter taste even if you use a full tablespoon in a recipe as baking soda alone would.

You can easily make homemade baking powder by combining:

- 2 tablespoons baking soda (alkaline base)

- 4 tablespoons cream of tartar (acid)

- 2 tablespoons cornstarch (filler)

GUAR GUM

Guar gum, which comes from a legume, has been used for centuries as a thickener and stabilizer in food and medicine. It works well in gluten-free baking to maintain the texture and structure of baked goods. It's also commonly found in store-bought almond milk, coconut milk, yogurts, body lotions, and fiber supplements. When digested, guar gum is fermented to short-chain fatty acids that do not appear to be absorbed by the gut. So basically, it passes quickly. The downside is some people may experience stomach-related discomfort from guar gum, including abdominal pain, cramps, diarrhea, and excess gas.

PSYLLIUM HUSK

This super fiber is a wonderful choice as a binder for baked goods and burgers. Plus, it's incredibly healthy. Made from the husks of the *Plantago ovata* plant's seeds, an important food for gut health, psyllium husk is good for digestion and is commonly known to be a laxative. It absorbs water in the gut and makes bowel movements easier. Not only that but it's also good for the heart and pancreas and provides prebiotics for the gut flora, allowing good bacteria to flourish. In foods, it absorbs liquid and swells, making dishes fluffy and binding ingredients together. It's recommended to use 8 ounces of fluids with every ½ to 2 teaspoon serving of psyllium to help absorb, bind, and thicken liquid.

XANTHAN GUM

A synthetic binder, xanthan gum is a polysaccharide (a carbohydrate) that is extracted from the bacteria *Xanthomonas campestris*. It is dried and turned into a powder and used in gluten-free cookies, muffins, cakes, breads, and pizza crust to help improve texture, consistency, and taste. Xanthan gum can also thicken syrup, ice cream, creamy salad dressings, and candy. The most common side effect of xanthan gum is an upset stomach caused by an altering of the gut bacteria. This can lead to increased bowel movements and loose stools. If you experience these symptoms, substitute 2 to 3 tablespoons psyllium husk powder for 1 teaspoon xanthan gum.

Gluten-Free Alternative Substitution Chart

To make it easier for you, you can return to this chart any time you may not have an ingredient on hand and are wondering what to use.

GLUTEN-FREE FLOUR (1 CUP)

1 cup almond flour
OR
½ cup brown rice flour + ¼ cup tapioca starch + ¼ cup potato starch
OR
¾ cup chickpea flour + ⅓ cup potato starch
OR
1 cup store-bought gluten-free flour mix (make sure it contains no dairy in the ingredient list)
OR
¾ cup almond flour + ¼ cup coconut flour

CORNSTARCH (½ CUP)

½ cup potato starch
OR
½ cup arrowroot starch or powder

TAPIOCA STARCH/FLOUR (1 CUP)

1 cup potato starch

BAKING POWDER

Make it by combining
4 tablespoons cream of tartar
2 tablespoons baking soda
2 tablespoons cornstarch or arrowroot

XANTHAN GUM

Equal amount of guar gum or carob (locust bean) gum
OR
gelatin (use powdered form). May also use 2 to 3 tablespoons psyllium husk for 1 teaspoon xanthan gum

PSYLLIUM HUSK

If you do not have psyllium husk on hand, use equal amounts of ground chia seeds or flaxseed meal

About the Recipes

It's time to get excited about preparing healthy, delicious, dairy- and gluten-free food! These dishes are full of ingredients to fuel your body the right way. It's a joy to be sharing my favorite family recipes for you to enjoy, too! Get ready to feel good again.

Whether you are a beginner cook or advanced in your culinary skills, these recipes are a fit for everyone. Each dish is designed to help folks acclimate to a gluten-free dairy-free diet and become confident in cooking recipes for this new way of eating. For the advanced cook, this book provides new ideas and savory options to expand your gluten-free dairy-free culinary skills and keep mealtime interesting.

Most of us don't have time for a lot of prep, involved recipes, or long cook times, so I've created the ultimate cookbook using ingredients that are affordable, easy to find, and healthy. Dinners are always on the table in 60 minutes or less from prep to cooking (unless it is slow cooking or roasting), or I give tips on how to make the meal faster.

Each recipe is labeled with potential food allergens and dietary styles, so look for the following labels: egg-free, tree nut-free, peanut-free, soy-free, vegetarian, or vegan. From my kitchen to yours, I am thrilled to share this book to help guide you in the right direction for healing, satisfying, and successful cooking.

Breakfast and Brunch

Sun-Dried Tomato Basil Frittata Muffins, page 29

Chickpea Pancakes with Maple Yogurt Topping and Berries

TREE NUT-FREE, PEANUT-FREE, SOY-FREE, VEGETARIAN

My family loves waking up on the weekends to the aroma of pancakes hot off the griddle. These are easy to make, and my kids could eat them all week long for breakfast, snacks, or dinner! They are made with chickpea flour bursting with protein and fiber to fuel you throughout the day. Make a triple batch and have leftovers all week long to use for peanut butter and honey sandwiches or for a quick breakfast on busy mornings.

- **Prep time: 15 minutes**
- **Cook time: 20 minutes**
- **Serves 4**

FOR THE PANCAKES

1 cup chickpea flour

½ cup potato starch

2½ teaspoons baking powder

¼ teaspoon salt (preferably pink Himalayan)

2 large eggs

1 cup nondairy milk

2 tablespoons extra-virgin olive oil

1 tablespoon maple syrup

1 tablespoon distilled white vinegar

FOR THE TOPPING

1 cup nondairy vanilla yogurt

2 tablespoons maple syrup

¼ teaspoon ground cinnamon

1 cup fresh berries, such as blueberries, raspberries, or chopped strawberries

TO MAKE THE PANCAKES

1. In a large bowl, combine the flour, potato starch, baking powder, and salt.

2. In a small bowl, whisk together the eggs, milk, oil, maple syrup, and vinegar. Pour over the flour mixture and stir just until combined. Let stand for 5 minutes. The batter may be slightly lumpy.

3. Lightly coat a griddle with non-stick cooking spray. Heat over medium heat.

4. Reduce the heat under the griddle to medium-low. Drop a scant ¼ cup of batter onto the griddle. Cook for 2 to 3 minutes, or until bubbles form. Flip and cook 2 minutes longer, or until golden brown. Repeat this process with the remaining batter.

TO MAKE THE TOPPING

1. In a small bowl, whisk together the yogurt, maple syrup and cinnamon.

2. Serve the pancakes warm with yogurt topping and fresh berries.

SUBSTITUTION TIP: Out of chickpea flour? Substitute 1 cup of almond flour. Almond flour still provides protein and fiber, and adds an extra dose of healthy fats.

Per Serving Calories: 335; Protein: 9g; Total carbohydrates: 45g; Sugars: 16g; Fiber: 4g; Total fat: 14g; Saturated fat: 2g; Cholesterol: 82mg; Sodium: 246mg

Tropical Pineapple Green Smoothie

EGG-FREE, TREE NUT-FREE, PEANUT-FREE, SOY-FREE, VEGAN

This fast and easy breakfast is like sipping dessert on a tropical island. It's an energizing meal packed with vitamin C, protein, iron, potassium, and omega-3 brain-boosting fats to help jump-start and energize the day! Short on time? Chop the ingredients (except the coconut water) and store in a sealed zip-top bag in the freezer. When you are ready to prepare, empty the contents into a blender, add the coconut water, and enjoy!

- **Prep time: 5 minutes**
- **Serves 1**

2 cups packed baby spinach

1 cup frozen pineapple cubes

½ banana, sliced and frozen

½ avocado

½ to ¾ cup coconut water

In a blender, combine the spinach, pineapple, banana, avocado, and ½ cup coconut water. Process until smooth and add up to ¼ cup more coconut water if needed.

VARIATION TIP: For a change of pace, substitute kale, beet greens, or chard leaves for the spinach. Be sure to remove the stems before adding to the blender.

Per Serving Calories: 316; Protein: 6g; Total carbohydrates: 49g; Sugars: 27g; Fiber: 12g; Total fat: 14g; Saturated fat: 2g; Cholesterol: 0mg; Sodium: 183mg

Fluffy Scrambled Eggs, Sausage, Spinach, and Mushroom Bowl

TREE NUT-FREE, PEANUT-FREE, SOY-FREE

Cozy up on the weekends with this savory breakfast that only takes one pan and 25 minutes! Simple and hearty with sausage, spices, and basil to bring out flavor, it's perfect for brunch or will become a favorite for Father's Day breakfast in bed!

- **Prep time: 10 minutes**
- **Cook time: 15 minutes**
- **Serves 4**

4 ounces bulk turkey sausage

½ teaspoon ground cumin

2 cups packed baby spinach

2 cups diced mushrooms

1 scallion, white and green parts, thinly sliced

2 tablespoons extra-virgin olive oil, divided

½ teaspoon salt (preferably pink Himalayan), divided

6 large eggs

2 tablespoons nondairy milk

Freshly ground black pepper

1 tablespoon chopped fresh basil

Salsa or ketchup, for topping (optional)

Fresh avocado slices, for topping (optional)

1. In a large nonstick skillet, cook the sausage and cumin over medium-high heat for 5 to 7 minutes, or until cooked through, breaking into tiny pieces with a wooden spoon. When fully cooked, add the spinach, mushrooms, and scallion and cook for 4 to 5 minutes, or until tender, adding 1 tablespoon of oil if necessary. Stir in ¼ teaspoon of salt. Cover and set aside.

2. In a large bowl, whisk together the eggs, milk, remaining ¼ teaspoon of salt, and pepper to taste for 30 seconds. This gets air flowing through and makes the eggs fluffy.

3. In a medium skillet, heat the remaining 1 tablespoon of olive oil over medium-low heat. Add the eggs and let sit for 1 minute without stirring. Then, with a wooden spoon or heatproof spatula, stir the eggs constantly until fully cooked. Remove from the heat and fold in the basil and the sausage mixture.

4. Serve topped with salsa or ketchup and fresh avocado slices (if using).

Per Serving (without toppings) Calories: 199; Protein: 13g; Total carbohydrates: 3g; Sugars: 2g; Fiber: 1g; Total fat: 16g; Saturated fat: 4g; Cholesterol: 259mg; Sodium: 529mg

Chocolate Chip Banana Bread Loaf

TREE NUT-FREE, PEANUT-FREE, SOY-FREE, VEGETARIAN

Warm your day with vanilla and cinnamon spices baked into a banana-sweetened bread that is loaded with melted chocolate chips. Quick breads make the perfect breakfast, snack, or dessert, especially when chocolate is involved!

- **Prep time: 15 minutes**
- **Cook time: 55 minutes**
- **Makes 1 loaf**

3 ripe bananas

2 cups all-purpose gluten-free flour

1 tablespoon baking powder

1 teaspoon ground cinnamon

½ teaspoon salt (preferably pink Himalayan)

2 large eggs

⅔ cup maple syrup

½ cup nondairy yogurt

1 tablespoon vanilla extract

1 cup dairy-free mini chocolate chips

1. Preheat the oven to 350°F. Line a 9-inch loaf pan with parchment paper so there is an overhang on two long sides.

2. In a small bowl, mash the bananas with a fork until creamy and blended.

3. In a medium bowl, combine the flour, baking powder, cinnamon, and salt.

4. In a large bowl, using an electric mixer, beat the eggs, maple syrup, yogurt, and vanilla on medium speed until well blended. Beat in the mashed bananas until combined. On low speed, beat in the flour mixture just until combined. Fold in ¾ cup of chocolate chips. Spoon the batter into the prepared pan. Sprinkle the remaining ¼ cup of chocolate chips over the top.

5. Bake for 50 to 60 minutes, or until a toothpick inserted in the center comes out clean. Let cool in the pan on a wire rack for 20 minutes, then remove by lifting the parchment paper. Transfer to the rack to cool completely. Wrap and store overnight for best slicing.

RECIPE TIP: Quick breads slice better the next day. Once the bread has cooled completely, wrap it tightly in parchment paper, then place in a sealed bag. Slice the next day and warm for 5 to 10 seconds in the microwave before serving.

Per Serving (1 slice) Calories: 265; Protein: 5g; Total carbohydrates: 52g; Sugars: 15g; Fiber: 3g; Total fat: 7g; Saturated fat: 4g; Cholesterol: 31mg; Sodium: 115mg

Chocolate Chip Oatmeal Chia Seed Muffins

TREE NUT-FREE, PEANUT-FREE, SOY-FREE, VEGETARIAN

These muffins are one of my most famous recipes. They're always a hit, especially for school groups and activities. My kids love them, readers love them, and you will, too! Not only do they have lovely cinnamon, vanilla, and chocolate flavors, but they're easy to make. Enjoy these healthy muffins loaded with oats and chia seeds and sweetened with a bit of honey any time of the day!

- **Prep time: 10 minutes**
- **Cook time: 20 minutes**
- **Makes 12 muffins**

2 large eggs

½ cup honey

¼ cup coconut oil, melted

1 teaspoon vanilla extract

1 cup all-purpose gluten-free flour

1 cup gluten-free quick-cooking oats

¼ cup flaxseed meal

2 tablespoons chia seeds

1 teaspoon ground cinnamon

1 teaspoon baking powder

½ teaspoon baking soda

½ teaspoon salt (preferably pink Himalayan)

½ cup unsweetened almond milk or coconut milk beverage

1 cup dairy-free chocolate chips

1. Preheat the oven to 350°F. Line a muffin pan with paper liners and coat the liners with nonstick cooking spray.

2. In a small bowl, whisk together the eggs, honey, coconut oil, and vanilla.

3. In a medium bowl, stir together the flour, oats, flaxseed meal, chia seeds, cinnamon, baking powder, baking soda, and salt. Pour the egg mixture into the flour mixture. Add the almond milk and stir together until well combined.

4. Carefully fold in the chocolate chips.

5. Evenly divide the mixture into the prepared muffin cups. Bake for 20 to 22 minutes, or until the tops are slightly browned. Let cool in the pan on a wire rack for 10 minutes, then transfer to the rack to cool completely. These muffins are best consumed within 3 days after baking.

VARIATION TIP: If you are not feeling like chocolate, substitute 1 cup of dried fruit such as raisins or cranberries for the chocolate chips.

Per Serving (1 muffin) Calories: 292; Protein: 6g; Total carbohydrates: 41g; Sugars: 12g; Fiber: 3g; Total fat: 14g; Saturated fat: 8g; Cholesterol: 27mg; Sodium: 173mg

Blueberry Oatmeal Muffins

PEANUT-FREE, SOY-FREE, VEGETARIAN

These warm, sweet, and fluffy muffins are bursting with blueberry and lemon flavor. This classic flavor combination is a convenient and delicious way to get heart-healthy fiber into your diet. I like to make these on the weekends for an easy breakfast or quick snack. Once cooled, store in an airtight container for up to 1 week.

- **Prep time: 10 minutes**
- **Cook time: 20 minutes**
- **Makes 12 muffins**

1 cup all-purpose gluten-free flour

1 cup gluten-free rolled oats

1 teaspoon baking powder

½ teaspoon baking soda

¾ teaspoon salt (preferably pink Himalayan)

2 large eggs

⅔ cup maple syrup

½ cup nondairy yogurt

¼ cup coconut oil, melted

¼ cup nondairy milk

1 teaspoon grated lemon zest

1 teaspoon vanilla extract

1 cup blueberries

1. Preheat the oven to 350°F. Line a muffin pan with paper liners and coat the liners with nonstick cooking spray.

2. In a large bowl, whisk together the flour, oats, baking powder, baking soda, and salt.

3. In a medium bowl, whisk together the eggs, maple syrup, yogurt, oil, milk, lemon zest, and vanilla until blended. Fold the egg mixture into the flour mixture just until moistened. Carefully fold in the blueberries. Let the batter stand for 5 minutes to soak the oats.

4. Evenly divide the mixture into the prepared muffin cups. Bake for 20 minutes, or until golden on top and a toothpick inserted in the center of a muffin comes out clean. Remove the muffins from the pan and transfer to a cooling rack to cool completely.

RECIPE TIP: Leaving the muffins in the warm pan will continue to cook them and may dry them out. To avoid this, take them out of the pan immediately after cooking. If they are too hot to touch, wait about 1 minute.

Per Serving (1 muffin) Calories: 185; Protein: 4g; Total carbohydrates: 28g; Sugars: 12g; Fiber: 1g; Total fat: 7g; Saturated fat: 4g; Cholesterol: 31mg; Sodium: 219mg

Peanut Butter and Chocolate Swirl Overnight Oats

EGG-FREE, SOY-FREE, VEGETARIAN

This is one of my favorite breakfasts to serve. It's effortless, takes little time to put together, and is loaded with chocolate and peanut butter flavors. I love waking up in the morning to a breakfast that is ready to serve and tastes like a dessert treat. For extra flavor and crunch, top each jar in the morning with a favorite jam, banana slices, and chopped nuts.

- **Prep time: 10 minutes plus overnight to set**
- **Serves 4**

2 cups gluten-free rolled oats

2 cups nondairy milk, plus more for serving

Salt (preferably pink Himalayan)

4 tablespoons organic peanut butter

4 tablespoons unsweetened cocoa powder

4 tablespoons honey or maple syrup

2 teaspoons ground cinnamon

4 tablespoons chopped peanuts or pecans

1. In each of four 16-ounce mason jars with lids, combine ½ cup of oats and ½ cup of milk. Mix until the oats are well coated. Sprinkle each with a dash of salt.

2. Top each jar with 1 tablespoon of peanut butter, 1 tablespoon of cocoa powder, 1 tablespoon of honey, and ½ teaspoon of cinnamon. Mix well.

3. Cover each jar with a lid and let it stand in the refrigerator overnight.

4. To serve, top each jar with 1 tablespoon of chopped nuts and extra milk. Enjoy chilled or warm.

VARIATION TIP: Instead of peanut butter you can use almond or cashew butter. If avoiding nuts, use sunflower seed butter and crunchy sunflower seeds to top.

Per Serving (without extra milk) Calories: 446; Protein: 18g; Total carbohydrates: 61g; Sugars: 24g; Fiber: 9g; Total fat: 18g; Saturated fat: 3g; Cholesterol: 0mg; Sodium: 178mg

Sun-Dried Tomato Basil Frittata Muffins

TREE NUT-FREE, PEANUT-FREE, SOY-FREE, VEGETARIAN

If you have 30 minutes, then you have time to make these easy egg muffins! They are light and fluffy and bursting with Italian flavors that are perfect for busy mornings. I love to make these at night so we have breakfast or a protein-packed snack ready to heat and eat. Having foods like these on hand is a great way to make healthier eating choices.

- **Prep time: 15 minutes**
- **Cook time: 15 minutes**
- **Makes 12 muffins**

12 large eggs

¼ teaspoon salt (preferably pink Himalayan)

¼ teaspoon freshly ground black pepper

1 cup packed baby spinach, finely chopped

½ cup sun-dried tomatoes in olive oil, drained and chopped

5 tablespoons green olive slices

1 scallion, green parts only, sliced

1 garlic clove, minced

2 tablespoons chopped fresh basil, divided

1. Preheat the oven to 350°F. Coat a silicone muffin pan with nonstick cooking spray or line a regular muffin pan with paper liners and coat the liners with nonstick cooking spray. Please note that this recipe works best with a silicone muffin pan.

2. In a large bowl, whisk together the eggs, salt, and pepper, getting air throughout the eggs. This makes the eggs fluffy.

3. Stir in the spinach, sun-dried tomatoes, olives, scallion, garlic, and 1 tablespoon of basil.

4. Evenly divide the mixture into the prepared muffin cups. Bake for 15 to 20 minutes, or until the centers are set. Let stand for about 5 minutes before serving. Remove from the pan and garnish with the remaining 1 tablespoon of basil. If desired, sprinkle with salt and pepper to taste.

VARIATION TIP: If you prefer a bit more protein (and even more delicious flavors), crumble 4 slices of cooked bacon into the egg mixture before pouring into the muffin cups.

Per Serving (1 muffin) Calories: 91; Protein: 6g; Total carbohydrates: 4g; Sugars: 2g; Fiber: 2g; Total fat: 5g; Saturated fat: 1g; Cholesterol: 164mg; Sodium: 361mg

Açai Smoothie Bowl

EGG-FREE, TREE NUT-FREE, PEANUT-FREE, SOY-FREE, VEGAN

Supercharge your mornings with this healthy and energizing superfood bowl that is rich in antioxidants! Not only is this easy to make, but it tastes like dessert. Top it with your favorite berries and seeds or turn it tropical by topping it with coconut flakes, kiwifruit, and mango chunks.

- **Prep time: 15 minutes**
- **Serves 2**

2 (3.5-ounce) packs frozen açai smoothie puree

1 cup frozen sliced strawberries

1 banana, fresh or frozen

¼ cup fresh spinach

½ to ¾ cup apple juice

TOPPINGS (OPTIONAL)

Banana slices

Sliced strawberries

Raspberries

Blueberries

Chopped nuts and seeds

Hemp seeds

Chia seeds

Honey

In a blender or food processor, combine the açai smoothie puree, strawberries, banana, spinach, and ½ cup of apple juice. Blend until smooth, adding more apple juice if needed. It should be very thick in consistency, but smooth, with no visible chunks. Divide between two bowls and sprinkle with the toppings of your choice (if using).

RECIPE TIP: When adding fruit as a topping, fresh is best. Make sure the bananas are not over- or underripe and berries are nice and firm, not mushy. Another nice fruit combination is kiwifruit slices and dried goji berries.

Per Serving (without toppings) Calories: 175; Protein: 2g; Total carbohydrates: 30g; Sugars: 19g; Fiber: 5g; Total fat: 6g; Saturated fat: 2g; Cholesterol: 0mg; Sodium: 17mg

Honey-Nut Granola

EGG-FREE, PEANUT-FREE, SOY-FREE, VEGETARIAN

One of the most epic ways to wake up in the morning is to a home filled with the sweet smells of warm homemade granola. It's like eating a bowl of crunchy bliss with sugary-vanilla flavors. Serve with nondairy milk or yogurt for breakfast. Or for dessert, use these crispy honeyed oats as a topping on fresh fruit or dairy-free ice cream.

- **Prep time: 10 minutes**
- **Cook time: 20 minutes**
- **Makes about 5 cups**

3 cups gluten-free rolled oats

¾ cup unsalted cashew pieces

¾ cup slivered almonds

½ cup honey

7 tablespoons coconut oil, melted (or nondairy butter, melted)

1 teaspoon vanilla extract

¼ teaspoon salt (preferably pink Himalayan)

⅓ cup dried fruit, such as raisins or cranberries

1. Preheat the oven to 325°F. Line a baking sheet with parchment paper.

2. In a large bowl, combine the oats, cashews, and almonds. Add the honey, oil, vanilla, and salt and toss to coat well.

3. Spread onto the prepared baking sheet. Bake for 25 to 30 minutes, or until golden brown, stirring occasionally to prevent burning. Set the pan on a wire rack to cool and immediately stir in the dried fruit.

4. Let cool to harden, then break into chunks before serving or storing. Store in an airtight container in a cool dry place.

RECIPE TIP: Let the granola cool completely. It will be soft when it first comes out of the oven and start to harden as it cools.

Per Serving (½ cup) Calories: 353; Protein: 7g; Total carbohydrates: 40g; Sugars: 18g; Fiber: 4g; Total fat: 20g; Saturated fat: 9g; Cholesterol: 0mg; Sodium: 61mg

Main-Dish Salads, Soups, and Grains

BLT Wedge Salad with Herb Cashew Dressing, page 39

Autumn Greens Salad with Dried Cranberries, Candied Walnuts, and Mustard Sherry Vinaigrette

EGG-FREE, PEANUT-FREE, SOY-FREE, VEGAN

. . . .

Tart and tangy flavors coat rich greens and crunchy nuts in this delicious salad that you'll love so much it will become a holiday staple. This dish is easy to put together, is vegetarian, and has just the right blend of textures. You can also top this salad with cooked salmon for a heartier meal.

. . . .

- **Prep time: 10 minutes**
- **Serves 4**

¼ cup extra-virgin olive oil

2 tablespoons dry sherry

2 teaspoons Dijon mustard

¼ cup chopped shallots

1 tablespoon chopped fresh oregano

¼ teaspoon salt (preferably pink Himalayan)

⅛ teaspoon freshly ground black pepper

3 cups mixed greens

¼ cup microgreens

⅓ cup dried cranberries

½ cup candied or glazed walnuts

1. In large bowl, whisk together the oil, sherry, mustard, shallots, oregano, salt, and pepper.

2. Add the mixed greens, microgreens, cranberries, and walnuts and toss to coat well. Serve immediately.

SUBSTITUTION TIP: If you do not have packaged mixed greens, use baby spinach or baby kale leaves instead. Use plain walnut pieces or pecan pieces for the candied walnuts, if desired.

Per Serving Calories: 251; Protein: 3g; Total carbohydrates: 13g; Sugars: 7g; Fiber: 3g; Total fat: 21g; Saturated fat: 3g; Cholesterol: 0mg; Sodium: 275mg

Arugula, Roasted Beets, Shaved Apple, Fennel, and Pistachio Salad with White Balsamic Dressing

EGG-FREE, PEANUT-FREE, SOY-FREE, VEGETARIAN

Here's a simple, sweet, and peppery salad that everyone will love! This refreshing winter salad is drizzled with a light vinaigrette that ramps up the flavors of fennel and apple. This hearty salad is packed full of nutrients thanks to the arugula and roasted beets, which help improve blood circulation, anemia, and cognitive function. It is best assembled just before serving to keep the beets from turning everything pink.

- **Prep time: 15 minutes**
- **Serves 4**

FOR THE SALAD

1 medium fennel bulb and fronds

1 large Honeycrisp apple, unpeeled

3 cups baby arugula

4 cooked beets, cut into 8 wedges

⅓ cup pistachios

FOR THE DRESSING

¼ cup extra-virgin olive oil

2 tablespoons white balsamic vinegar

2 teaspoons honey

2 teaspoons Dijon mustard

1 garlic clove, crushed in a garlic press

1 tablespoon minced fennel fronds

Salt (preferably pink Himalayan)

Freshly ground black pepper

TO MAKE THE SALAD

Remove the fennel fronds, mince, and set aside. With a knife or mandoline, thinly slice the apple and fennel and place in a large bowl. Add the arugula, beets, and pistachios.

TO MAKE THE DRESSING

1. In a small bowl, whisk together the oil, vinegar, honey, mustard, garlic, and fennel fronds.

2. Pour the dressing over the salad and toss to coat well. If desired, season with salt and pepper to taste. Serve immediately.

INGREDIENT TIP: This salad looks festive with ribbons of apple. You can do this by using a vegetable peeler and working down the sides of the apple for slender slices.

Per Serving Calories: 295; Protein: 4g; Total carbohydrates: 26g; Sugars: 17g; Fiber: 5g; Total fat: 21g; Saturated fat: 3g; Cholesterol: 0mg; Sodium: 287mg

Shredded Chicken Spa Salad with Orange Champagne Dressing

EGG-FREE, TREE NUT-FREE, PEANUT-FREE, SOY-FREE

Imagine sitting poolside at a luxury hotel enjoying one of the most refreshing salads of your life! That's the inspiration behind this delicious dish. Crunchy and loaded with mouthwatering texture and subtly sweet juices, it'll have your taste buds yearning for more. The best part is that this salad is packed with protein to energize your body and help you feel lean and clean throughout the day.

- **Prep time: 15 minutes**
- **Serves 4**

½ cup extra-virgin olive oil

3 tablespoons orange champagne vinegar

2 tablespoons honey

1 teaspoon Dijon mustard

½ teaspoon salt (preferably pink Himalayan)

¼ teaspoon freshly ground black pepper

6 cups chopped romaine lettuce

6 cups chopped Belgian endive (red or green)

2 cups shredded rotisserie chicken

1 cup diced cucumber

1 cup chopped pecans

½ cup diced red onion

½ cup pomegranate seeds

Mint leaves, for garnish

1. In a large bowl, whisk together the oil, vinegar, honey, mustard, salt, and pepper.

2. Add the lettuce, endive, chicken, cucumber, pecans, onion, and pomegranate seeds and toss to coat well.

3. Garnish with mint leaves and serve immediately.

RECIPE TIP: This is a great salad to make with leftovers. Have leftover grilled chicken in the house? Dice it and serve cold or warm on top of the salad.

Per Serving Calories: 632; Protein: 25g; Total carbohydrates: 27g; Sugars: 17g; Fiber: 7g; Total fat: 50g; Saturated fat: 7g; Cholesterol: 55mg; Sodium: 366mg

Spanish Chicken Caesar Salad with Cilantro Dressing

EGG-FREE, PEANUT-FREE, SOY-FREE

This recipe is inspired by a combination of my favorite Mexican flavors and traditional Caesar dressing, but made without the dairy. I love the pungent flavor capers add to the dressing in place of anchovies. The dressing is also great served over roasted vegetables and Buddha bowls.

- **Prep time: 20 minutes**
- **Serves 4**

FOR THE DRESSING

1 cup cashews

½ cup water

½ avocado

1 large handful fresh cilantro, stems included

2 tablespoons freshly squeezed lemon juice

¼ cup capers, drained

2 garlic cloves

½ teaspoon salt (preferably pink Himalayan)

¼ teaspoon freshly ground black pepper

FOR THE SALAD

6 cups chopped romaine lettuce

2 cups shredded roasted chicken

1 cup corn kernels

1 cup diced peeled jicama

1 red bell pepper, diced

⅓ cup hulled pumpkin seeds

TO MAKE THE DRESSING

In a food processor, combine the cashews, water, avocado, cilantro, lemon juice, capers, garlic, salt, and pepper. Pulse until smooth, adding more water, 1 tablespoon at a time, if needed to thin the dressing.

TO MAKE THE SALAD

In a large bowl, combine the lettuce, chicken, corn, jicama, bell pepper, and pumpkin seeds. Top with the dressing and toss to coat well. Serve immediately.

INGREDIENT TIP: For a creamier and smoother texture in the dressing, soak the cashews in 3 cups of water in the refrigerator for 3 hours. Drain and add them to the food processor with the dressing ingredients.

Per Serving Calories: 535; Protein: 17g; Total carbohydrates: 70g; Sugars: 11g; Fiber: 13g; Total fat: 26g; Saturated fat: 4g; Cholesterol: 28mg; Sodium: 352mg

Quinoa Citrus Salad

EGG-FREE, PEANUT-FREE, SOY-FREE, VEGAN

A summer potluck favorite! This delicious grain salad is bursting with flavor from the fresh citrus fruits. Change it up by topping with chopped pecans or your favorite fish fillet.

- **Prep time: 15 minutes**
- **Cook time: 15 minutes**
- **Serves 4**

½ cup quinoa

1 cup water

¼ cup orange juice

4 teaspoons freshly squeezed lime juice

3 tablespoons avocado oil

½ teaspoon chili powder

½ teaspoon salt (preferably pink Himalayan)

¼ teaspoon freshly ground black pepper

1 (10-ounce) bag baby arugula

1 navel orange, peeled and diced

1 red grapefruit, peeled and cut into sections

1 avocado, peeled, pitted, and cut into 1-inch pieces

½ cup almond slices

1. In a medium saucepan, combine the quinoa and water and cook according to package directions.
2. Meanwhile, in a small bowl, whisk together the orange juice, lime juice, oil, chili powder, salt, and pepper.
3. On four plates, evenly divide the arugula, quinoa, orange, grapefruit, avocados, and almonds. Drizzle with the dressing and serve immediately.

SUBSTITUTION TIP: This versatile dish works well with cooked rice or buckwheat in place of quinoa. For a twist on flavor, change up the fruit by substituting peaches and plums for the grapefruit and orange.

Per Serving Calories: 391; Protein: 10g; Total carbohydrates: 34g; Sugars: 10g; Fiber: 9g; Total fat: 27g; Saturated fat: 3g; Cholesterol: 0mg; Sodium: 318mg

BLT Wedge Salad with Herb Cashew Dressing

EGG-FREE, SOY-FREE

This is a family favorite salad that my husband and I love to enjoy on date night. When going dairy-free, giving up flavorful blue cheese, which is typical on this salad, is challenging. Here a delicious herb-infused cashew dressing provides punches of flavor and complements the bacon pieces. Try adding sunflower seeds or walnuts for more texture.

- **Prep time: 15 minutes**
- **Cook time: 15 minutes**
- **Serves 4**

4 slices bacon (pork or turkey)

1 cup cashews, raw and unsalted

½ cup water

1 large handful fresh cilantro, stems included

1 large handful fresh basil, stems included

Juice of 1 lemon

1 shallot, peeled and halved

½ teaspoon salt (preferably pink Himalayan)

½ teaspoon freshly ground black pepper

1 head iceberg lettuce, cored and quartered

2 Roma or plum tomatoes, seeded and diced

1. In a skillet, cook the bacon over medium-high heat for 8 to 12 minutes, turning frequently, until crispy. Place a paper towel on a plate and top with the cooked bacon. Place another paper towel on top and pat to absorb any extra oil. Once cooled, crumble the bacon into pieces.

2. In a food processor, combine the cashews, water, cilantro, basil, lemon, shallot, salt, and pepper. Pulse the dressing until smooth, adding more water, 1 tablespoon at a time, if needed.

3. On each of four plates, place 1 lettuce wedge. Drizzle with the dressing. Top each with one-quarter of the bacon and tomatoes. Serve immediately.

INGREDIENT TIP: For a creamier and smoother texture in the dressing, soak the cashews in 3 cups of water in the refrigerator for 3 hours. Drain and add them to the food processor with the other dressing ingredients.

Per Serving Calories: 220; Protein: 10g; Total carbohydrates: 10g; Sugars: 3g; Fiber: 2g; Total fat: 16g; Saturated fat: 4g; Cholesterol: 21mg; Sodium: 739mg

Skinny Roasted Vegetable Quinoa Salad

EGG-FREE, TREE NUT-FREE, PEANUT-FREE, SOY-FREE, VEGAN

This well-rounded salad is simple enough to make even for a beginner chef. Roasting vegetables brings out their natural sweetness and complements the nutty flavor of quinoa and the bite of the spinach. This is a great dish to meal prep and have as a healthy lunch. Divide among airtight food storage containers and refrigerate for up to 5 days.

- **Prep time: 10 minutes**
- **Cook time: 20 minutes**
- **Serves 4**

1 red bell pepper

1 green bell pepper

1 yellow bell pepper

1½ cups cherry tomatoes

3 garlic cloves

½ red onion

1 tablespoon balsamic vinegar

2 cups water

1 cup quinoa

¼ cup extra-virgin olive oil

Juice of 2 limes

2 teaspoons ground cumin

½ teaspoon salt (preferably pink Himalayan)

¼ teaspoon freshly ground black pepper

4 cups baby spinach

1 (15-ounce) can black beans, drained and rinsed

1 avocado, peeled, pitted, and chopped

¼ cup chopped fresh cilantro

1. Preheat the oven 400°F. Line a rimmed baking sheet with parchment paper.

2. Place the whole red, green, and yellow peppers, tomatoes, garlic, and onion on the prepared baking sheet. Drizzle with the vinegar and toss to coat. Cover loosely with aluminum foil. Bake for 20 minutes, or until tender and slightly charred. Remove from the oven, uncover, and let cool.

3. Meanwhile, in a medium saucepan over medium-high heat, bring the water and quinoa to a boil. Reduce the heat to medium-low, cover, and simmer for 15 minutes, or until the quinoa is tender and the water is absorbed. Fluff with a fork and set aside to cool.

4. In a large bowl, whisk together the oil, lime juice, cumin, salt, and black pepper.

5. Once the roasted vegetables have cooled, seed and dice the peppers, dice the onion, and mince the garlic. Add to the bowl with the dressing. Add the cooked quinoa, spinach, beans, avocado, and cilantro. If desired, season with more salt and black pepper to taste. Gently toss to coat well. Serve immediately or chill to serve later.

SIMPLIFY IT: To assemble this salad quickly, roast the vegetables up to 2 days ahead, dice them and drizzle with a bit of oil, then store in an airtight container. The quinoa may also be made in advance and placed in an airtight container. Store both in the refrigerator.

Per Serving Calories: 399 ; Protein: 15g; Total carbohydrates: 58g; Sugars: 6g; Fiber: 15g; Total fat: 13g; Saturated fat: 3g; Cholesterol: 0mg; Sodium: 339mg

Slow Cooker Creamy Corn Chowder

EGG-FREE, TREE NUT-FREE, PEANUT-FREE, SOY-FREE, VEGAN

This elegant and creamy vegan corn chowder is perfect for fall entertaining. Reminiscent of seafood chowder, it's dairy-free and is made with sweet corn kernels and potatoes instead of seafood. It's comforting, slightly sweet, and simple to prepare. Enjoy it chunky or pureed to a smooth and creamy texture.

- **Prep time: 15 minutes**
- **Cook time: 4 hours**
- **Serves 4**

2 (16-ounce) bags organic frozen corn

2 cups diced Yukon Gold potatoes

1 white onion, diced

1 red bell pepper, diced

1 carrot, diced

2 garlic cloves, minced

4 cups vegetable broth

1 tablespoon chopped fresh parsley

1 tablespoon chopped fresh chives

1 tablespoon chopped fresh thyme

3 tablespoons cornstarch

1 teaspoon salt (preferably pink Himalayan)

1 teaspoon paprika

½ teaspoon ground white pepper

1½ cups canned full-fat coconut milk

Hot sauce, for serving (optional)

1. In a slow cooker, combine the corn, potatoes, onion, bell pepper, carrot, garlic, broth, parsley, chives, thyme, cornstarch, salt, paprika, and white pepper. Cook on low for 3½ hours, or until the potatoes are soft.

2. Add the coconut milk and let cook for about 30 minutes more. Enjoy chunky, or puree in a food processor or blender (or with an immersion blender). If desired, serve with hot sauce.

SUBSTITUTION TIP: In place of the fresh herbs, use 1 teaspoon each of dried parsley, chives, and thyme.

Per Serving Calories: 490; Protein: 11g; Total carbohydrates: 70g; Sugars: 16g; Fiber: 8g; Total fat: 21g; Saturated fat: 17g; Cholesterol: 0mg; Sodium: 634mg

Hearty Vegetable Soup

EGG-FREE, TREE NUT-FREE, PEANUT-FREE, SOY-FREE, VEGAN

This vegetable soup is healthy and ready in less than 30 minutes! Using frozen vegetables cuts the prep time in half and makes it a cinch to whip up this soup at a moment's notice. It's one of my kids' favorites and a great way to ensure they're eating vegetables.

- **Prep time: 10 minutes**
- **Cook time: 20 minutes**
- **Serves 4**

1 (26-ounce) carton or can diced tomatoes, undrained

1 (16-ounce) bag frozen mixed vegetables (green beans, corn, peas, and carrots)

3 cups vegetable broth, divided

Juice of 1 lemon

1 celery stalk, diced

½ onion, diced

½ cup chopped fresh parsley

2 teaspoons ground cumin

1 bay leaf

½ teaspoon salt (preferably pink Himalayan)

¼ teaspoon freshly ground black pepper

1. In a large saucepan, combine the tomatoes, vegetables, 2 cups of broth, the lemon juice, celery, onion, parsley, cumin, bay leaf, salt, and pepper. Cover and cook over high heat until the edges of the soup start to bubble.

2. Reduce the heat to medium-low, cover, and simmer for 20 minutes, or until the vegetables are soft, adding more of the broth if a thinner soup is desired.

VARIATION TIP: Try adding noodles to the soup for an even heartier meal. About 10 minutes before the soup is done, add 1 cup uncooked gluten-free elbow noodles and cook until al dente, adding more broth if needed.

Per Serving Calories: 137; Protein: 6g; Total carbohydrates: 26g; Sugars: 7g; Fiber: 4g; Total fat: 0g; Saturated fat: 0g; Cholesterol: 0mg; Sodium: 765mg

Southwest Rice and Bean Bowls

EGG-FREE, TREE NUT-FREE, PEANUT-FREE, SOY-FREE, VEGAN

Earthy and zesty flavors of beans, lime, salty olives, and a sweet punch of red bell pepper fill this skillet dish. This easy medley is so versatile it can be served as a side dish, a taco salad with chips, or a main dish topped with cooked chicken, fish, or steak.

- **Prep time: 10 minutes**
- **Cook time: 10 minutes**
- **Serves 4**

3 cups cooked brown rice

2 cups fresh or frozen and thawed corn kernels

1 (15-ounce) can black beans, drained and rinsed

1 (15-ounce) can fire-roasted tomatoes, drained

1 red bell pepper, finely diced

1 poblano pepper, seeded and finely diced

1 jalapeño pepper, seeded and finely diced

2 teaspoons chili powder

2 scallions, white and green parts, finely diced

½ cup finely chopped fresh cilantro

¼ cup green olives, finely chopped

3 tablespoons freshly squeezed lime juice

2 tablespoons extra-virgin olive oil

Salt (preferably pink Himalayan)

Freshly ground black pepper

FOR SERVING (OPTIONAL)
Fresh salsa

Avocado slices

Gluten-free tortilla chips

1. In a large skillet over medium-low heat, cook the rice, corn, beans, tomatoes, peppers, and chili powder, stirring occasionally, for 7 to 10 minutes or until heated through.

2. Stir in the scallions, cilantro, olives, lime juice, and oil. If desired, add salt and pepper to taste.

3. Evenly divide among four bowls. If desired, top each with fresh salsa and avocado slices and serve with tortilla chips.

SUBSTITUTION TIP: Swap pinto or red kidney beans for the black beans for variety. You can also use a green bell pepper in place of a poblano pepper, although the earthy flavor of poblano is my favorite.

Per Serving (without toppings or chips)
Calories: 333; Protein: 10g;
Total carbohydrates: 53g; Sugars: 7g;
Fiber: 10g; Total fat: 10g; Saturated fat: 1g;
Cholesterol: 0mg; Sodium: 266mg

Chicken Tortilla Soup

EGG-FREE, TREE NUT-FREE, PEANUT-FREE, SOY-FREE

This is one of my favorite recipes since it comes together well with delicious hearty ingredients. The secrets to this soup are the green chiles and chili powder, which add loads of flavor. I typically skip adding a jalapeño pepper as it's too spicy for my kids, but you can add a diced, seeded one for extra heat if desired.

- **Prep time: 15 minutes**
- **Cook time: 34 minutes**
- **Serves 4**

2 tablespoons extra-virgin olive oil

1 medium onion, diced

1 Anaheim pepper, seeded and finely diced

1 garlic clove, minced

1 teaspoon chili powder

1½ teaspoons ground coriander

4 cups chicken or vegetable broth

2 (15-ounce) cans fire-roasted diced tomatoes, undrained

1 (15-ounce) can black beans, drained and rinsed

1 (4-ounce) can diced green chiles, undrained

1 cup fresh or frozen and thawed corn kernels

2 cups shredded cooked chicken breast

¼ cup chopped fresh cilantro, for garnish

Fresh avocado slices, for serving (optional)

Salt (preferably pink Himalayan)

Freshly ground black pepper

1. In a large saucepan, heat the oil over medium-high heat. Add the onion, Anaheim pepper, garlic, chili powder, and coriander and cook for 3 to 4 minutes, or until the onion and pepper are tender.

2. Add the broth, tomatoes with their juices, black beans, green chiles with their juices, corn, and chicken. Bring to a boil, reduce the heat to low, cover, and simmer for 30 minutes to blend the flavors.

3. Garnish with fresh cilantro. Serve with avocado slices (if using). Season with salt and pepper to taste.

SUBSTITUTION TIP: If you have trouble finding an Anaheim pepper, you can opt for a green bell pepper instead without altering the flavor much.

Per Serving (without avocado) Calories: 406; Protein: 30g; Total carbohydrates: 42g; Sugars: 11g; Fiber: 11g; Total fat: 13g; Saturated fat: 3g; Cholesterol: 53mg; Sodium: 1,300mg

Cream of Cauliflower Soup

EGG-FREE, TREE NUT-FREE, PEANUT-FREE, SOY-FREE, VEGAN

A creamy, delicious white soup made with a cauliflower and cashew milk base. Nutmeg complements the nutty, bitter flavors of the cauliflower. For a little texture, set aside some cauliflower chunks before pureeing into a smooth texture, then stir them in at the end.

- **Prep time: 15 minutes**
- **Cook time: 15 minutes**
- **Serves 6**

4 tablespoons nondairy butter

1 large head cauliflower, broken into small florets

1 large shallot, diced

2 cups vegetable broth, divided

1½ cups unsweetened cashew milk or coconut milk beverage

1 teaspoon salt (preferably pink Himalayan)

½ teaspoon freshly ground black pepper

½ teaspoon ground turmeric

¼ teaspoon ground cumin

¼ teaspoon ground nutmeg

½ cup cornstarch

2 tablespoons nutritional yeast

1. In a large saucepan, melt the butter over medium-high heat. Add the cauliflower and shallot and cook for 5 minutes, or until softened. Stir in 1 cup of broth, the cashew milk, salt, pepper, turmeric, cumin, and nutmeg. Bring to a simmer.

2. Meanwhile, in a small bowl, whisk together the remaining 1 cup of broth and the cornstarch until thick and creamy.

3. Add the cornstarch slurry to the simmering broth, stirring until blended. Reduce the heat to low and simmer, uncovered, for 10 minutes, or until thickened.

4. Working in batches if necessary, transfer the soup to a blender or food processor, and puree. Return the soup to the saucepan and stir in the nutritional yeast.

INGREDIENT TIP: For a richer flavor, roast the cauliflower first. Toss the florets in olive oil and sprinkle with salt and pepper. Roast in a 400°F oven for about 20 minutes, or until golden. In step 1, cook the shallot, then add the roasted cauliflower with the broth.

Per Serving Calories: 190; Protein: 6g; Total carbohydrates: 20g; Sugars: 4g; Fiber: 4g; Total fat: 10g; Saturated fat: 2g; Cholesterol: 0mg; Sodium: 621mg

Mediterranean Quinoa Salad

EGG-FREE, TREE NUT-FREE, PEANUT-FREE, SOY-FREE, VEGAN

This satisfying, healthy, and easy quinoa salad full of chopped cucumbers, juicy grape tomatoes, salty olives, and tender chickpeas is so flavorful tossed in an aromatic herb-infused olive oil dressing. Serve it at your next barbecue, afternoon brunch, or dinner party.

- **Prep time: 15 minutes**
- **Serves 4**

½ cup extra-virgin olive oil

Juice of 1 lemon

2 tablespoons red wine vinegar

1 teaspoon Dijon mustard

1 teaspoon coconut sugar

1 teaspoon dried oregano

½ teaspoon salt (preferably pink Himalayan)

¼ teaspoon freshly ground black pepper

2 cups cooked quinoa

2 cups chopped spinach

1 (15-ounce) can chickpeas, drained and rinsed

1 cup grape tomatoes, halved

1 cucumber, quartered and sliced

20 green olives, sliced

½ red onion, thinly sliced

1 tablespoon chopped fresh parsley

1. In a large bowl, whisk together the oil, lemon juice, vinegar, mustard, coconut sugar, oregano, salt, and pepper.

2. Add the quinoa, spinach, chickpeas, tomatoes, cucumber, olives, and onion to the bowl and toss to combine. Garnish with the parsley.

SIMPLIFY IT: I like to cook a large batch of quinoa each week and keep it in the refrigerator. This makes the base for a quick meal and saves valuable time. Make the quinoa in advance according to the package directions and cool before storing in an airtight container.

Per Serving Calories: 562; Protein: 11g; Total carbohydrates: 49g; Sugars: 6g; Fiber: 11g; Total fat: 35g; Saturated fat: 5g; Cholesterol: 0mg; Sodium: 1,290mg

Coconut Curry Chicken and Rice Soup

EGG-FREE, PEANUT-FREE, SOY-FREE

This flavorful blend of Asian spices, chicken, rice, ginger, and lime will not only have your taste buds singing but may help reduce inflammation and ease joint and arthritis pain thanks to the magic of turmeric and ginger. These powerful ingredients also help detox the liver, improve skin health, boost immunity, and support weight loss.

- **Prep time: 15 minutes**
- **Cook time: 25 minutes**
- **Serves 4**

3 cups vegetable broth

1 (15-ounce) can full-fat coconut milk

2 cups chopped chard or kale stems (reserve the leaves for another recipe)

½ cup diced red onion

½ cup diced celery

½ cup diced carrot

2 stalks fresh lemongrass, cut into several pieces, or grated zest of 1 lemon

1 (1-inch) piece fresh ginger, grated

1 garlic clove, minced

1 teaspoon garam masala

½ teaspoon ground turmeric

½ teaspoon salt (preferably pink Himalayan)

¼ teaspoon freshly ground black pepper

1½ tablespoons sugar

½ cup white rice

2 cups cooked cubed or shredded chicken breast

Juice of 2 limes

¾ cup chopped fresh cilantro

Chili powder (optional), for a little kick

1. In a large stockpot, combine the broth, coconut milk, chard stems, onion, celery, carrot, lemongrass, ginger, garlic, garam masala, turmeric, salt, pepper, and sugar. Bring to a simmer over medium-high heat.

2. Reduce the heat to low, stir in the rice, cover, and simmer for 20 minutes, or until the rice is cooked. Discard the lemongrass.

3. Remove from the heat and stir in the chicken, lime juice, and cilantro. Cover and let stand for 5 minutes.

4. Evenly divide among four bowls. Garnish with a pinch of chili powder (if using).

VARIATION TIP: For a lighter, lower-fat soup, use canned lite coconut milk. It has a higher percentage of water to coconut fat, reducing the calories and fat grams. Of course, using lite coconut milk will make the soup slightly less thick, creamy, and rich.

Per Serving Calories: 484; Protein: 25g; Total carbohydrates: 32g; Sugars: 8g; Fiber: 2g; Total fat: 30g; Saturated fat: 23g; Cholesterol: 62mg; Sodium: 522mg

Mushroom Asparagus Risotto with White Truffle Oil

EGG-FREE, TREE NUT-FREE, PEANUT-FREE, SOY-FREE, VEGAN

White truffle oil is a favorite condiment of mine that pops up in stores during the cooler months. It pairs perfectly with earthy foods like cauliflower, asparagus, and mushrooms and is delicious drizzled over pasta and rice dishes. In college I waitressed at a fancy restaurant where they would serve the staff a divine truffle oil mac and cheese. Now I use the oil in risotto, which gives this comforting gluten-free dish a burst of aromatic intensity.

- **Prep time: 15 minutes**
- **Cook time: 35 minutes**
- **Serves 6–8**

4 tablespoons nondairy butter, divided

1 white onion, minced

2 cups finely chopped mushrooms

2 cups diced asparagus

1½ cups Arborio rice

4 cups vegetable or chicken broth

½ cup dry white wine

Salt (preferably pink Himalayan)

Freshly ground black pepper

4 tablespoons white truffle oil

⅓ cup shredded nondairy Parmesan cheese

2 tablespoons chopped fresh parsley

1. In a large saucepan, heat 3 tablespoons of butter over medium heat. Add the onion, mushrooms, and asparagus and cook, stirring often, for 10 minutes, or until softened. Stir in the rice.

2. Add the broth, wine, and a dash of salt and pepper. Bring to a simmer over medium-high heat. Reduce the heat to low, cover, and simmer for 22 minutes, or until the rice is cooked through. The texture should be creamy, not soupy or mushy.

3. If desired, season with salt and pepper to taste. Stir in the remaining 1 tablespoon of butter, the white truffle oil, cheese, and parsley.

VARIATION TIP: Including nuts in vegetarian dishes is a delicious way to add texture and protein. You can sprinkle chopped pecans right on top of this risotto before serving as a nutrient bonus.

Per Serving Calories: 610; Protein: 13g; Total carbohydrates: 66g; Sugars: 4g; Fiber: 5g; Total fat: 31g; Saturated fat: 5g; Cholesterol: 0mg; Sodium: 744mg

Pastas and Stir-Fries

Healthy Summer Spaghetti, page 70

Vegetable Lasagna

PEANUT-FREE, SOY-FREE, VEGETARIAN

This tasty family dinner is packed with mushrooms, onions, and zucchini. I like to prepare it in the morning, bake and cool it, and then refrigerate it until it's time to reheat for dinner. To reheat it, simply cook it covered in the oven at 300°F for 20 to 30 minutes, or until the center is heated through. Or completely assemble ahead of time (without baking) and then cook fully right before dinner time.

- **Prep time: 15 minutes**
- **Cook time: 1 hour, plus 50 minutes to rest**
- **Serves 8**

1 (9- to 10-ounce) package gluten-free lasagna noodles

2 tablespoons extra-virgin olive oil

2 cups sliced mushrooms

1 large white onion, diced

1 large zucchini, diced

1 yellow squash, diced

Salt (preferably pink Himalayan)

Freshly ground black pepper

2 cups Vegan Ricotta Cheese (page 166)

4 tablespoons unsweetened cashew milk

2 large eggs

2 teaspoons dried oregano

2 teaspoons dried basil

1 (25-ounce) jar marinara sauce

2 cups shredded nondairy mozzarella cheese

1. Cook the noodles according to package directions. Coat a 9-by-13-inch baking dish with nonstick cooking spray.

2. In a medium saucepan, heat the oil over medium-low heat. Add the mushrooms, onion, zucchini, squash, and a dash of salt and pepper. Cook, stirring often, for 10 minutes, or until the mushrooms start to soften and the onion becomes translucent. Set aside.

3. In a large bowl, stir together the ricotta cheese, milk, eggs, oregano, and basil.

4. Spread about one-quarter of the marinara sauce on the bottom of the prepared baking dish. Place one-quarter of the noodles in a single layer over the sauce. Spread with one-third of the ricotta mixture, then top with one-third of the vegetables. Repeat the layers two more times, starting with tomato sauce, then noodles, ricotta mixture, and vegetables. Before arranging the fourth layer of noodles, dip the noodles in water, then top with the remaining tomato sauce and the shredded mozzarella.

5. Let the lasagna sit for 30 minutes to allow the noodles to absorb the liquid and the flavors to set. Meanwhile, preheat the oven to 375°F.

6. Bake for 40 minutes, or until the cheese is browned and bubbling and the center is hot. If the sides start to burn, cover with aluminum foil, then remove the foil for the last 5 minutes of cooking. Let rest for 20 minutes before serving.

INGREDIENT TIP: I like to use cashew milk for its thickness, and it pairs well with the ricotta. But feel free to use almond milk or coconut milk instead.

Per Serving Calories: 417; Protein: 13g; Total carbohydrates: 44g; Sugars: 6g; Fiber: 7g; Total fat: 20g; Saturated fat: 4g; Cholesterol: 45mg; Sodium: 595mg

Vegan Butternut Squash Mac and Cheese

EGG-FREE, TREE NUT-FREE, PEANUT-FREE, SOY-FREE, VEGAN

A delicious, homestyle, comforting meal that is wonderful in the fall and winter months when butternut squash is in season. It's a great way to ensure that you and the family are getting vitamin A–rich vegetables (and for those who don't love squash, they may never know it is pureed into the creamy sauce). To make the recipe faster, cook the squash in advance and have it ready to quickly puree and add to the noodles.

- **Prep time: 15 minutes**
- **Cook time: 55 minutes**
- **Serves 6**

1 medium butternut squash, peeled, seeded, and cut into 1-inch cubes

1 tablespoon extra-virgin olive oil

1 small onion

2 garlic cloves

1 cup cashew milk, plus ¼ cup (if needed)

¼ cup nutritional yeast

2 tablespoons nondairy butter

1 tablespoon Dijon mustard

¾ teaspoon salt (preferably pink Himalayan)

¼ teaspoon freshly ground black pepper

1 (16-ounce) package gluten-free elbow macaroni

1. Preheat the oven to 400°F.

2. Place the butternut squash on a rimmed baking sheet and drizzle with the oil, tossing to coat. Add a drizzle of water to the pan. Wrap the onion and garlic cloves in a piece of aluminum foil and place on the pan. Roast for 45 minutes, or until the squash is tender. Remove from the oven and let cool slightly.

3. In a blender, combine the squash, onion, garlic, 1 cup of milk, the nutritional yeast, butter, mustard, salt, and pepper. Blend until smooth and creamy. For a thinner sauce, add about ¼ cup more milk in increments until the desired texture is achieved.

4. Meanwhile, in a soup pot, cook the noodles according to package directions. Drain the noodles and return to the pot.

5. Pour the squash sauce over the drained noodles. If desired, add extra salt and pepper to taste. Toss to coat well.

SUBSTITUTION TIP: To keep this recipe as classic as possible, I use elbow macaroni, but any small shape of gluten-free pasta, such as penne, rotini, or farfalle, will work just as well.

Per Serving Calories: 391; Protein: 9g; Total carbohydrates: 73g; Sugars: 3g; Fiber: 5g; Total fat: 8g; Saturated fat: 2g; Cholesterol: 0mg; Sodium: 429mg

Artichoke and Lemon Pasta

EGG-FREE, PEANUT-FREE, SOY-FREE

Citrus notes pair with the nutty artichoke flavors and add just the right contrast to this pasta dish.

- **Prep time: 15 minutes**
- **Cook time: 30 minutes**
- **Serves 8**

4 tablespoons nondairy butter

2 (15-ounce) cans baby artichokes, drained and quartered

Grated zest and juice of 1 lemon

2 shallots, minced

½ cup cornstarch

1 cup chicken broth

1½ cups cashew milk

¼ cup nutritional yeast

1 (12-ounce) package gluten-free spaghetti

½ cup toasted pine nuts

1 cup frozen peas, thawed

2 teaspoons fresh thyme leaves

¼ cup capers, drained

Salt (preferably pink Himalayan)

Freshly ground black pepper

1 tablespoon fresh parsley

1. In a large saucepan, heat the butter over medium heat. Add the artichokes, lemon zest, lemon juice, and shallots and cook for 5 minutes, stirring, until lightly browned. Stir in the cornstarch to form a paste, then add the broth, milk, and nutritional yeast, stirring constantly until thickened.

2. Cook the spaghetti according to package directions. Reserve ½ cup pasta water. Drain well.

3. Add the drained spaghetti, pine nuts, peas, thyme, and capers to the artichoke mixture and toss to coat well. Add the reserved pasta water as needed. Top with a light sprinkle of salt and pepper and garnish with fresh parsley.

VARIATION TIP: For a hearty, protein-rich meal, serve with chicken or salmon. Or stir a can of drained and rinsed chickpeas into the mixture while adding the cooked pasta.

Per Serving Calories: 358; Protein: 9g; Total carbohydrates: 54g; Sugars: 4g; Fiber: 5g; Total fat: 13g; Saturated fat: 2g; Cholesterol: 1mg; Sodium: 615mg

Healthy Chana Masala

EGG-FREE, PEANUT-FREE, SOY-FREE, VEGAN

This is an easy, 30-minute, Indian-inspired meal that features comforting notes of curry spices in a tomato-based dish. Simmer the components together, then serve it with rice. Or serve with a side of roasted potatoes and vegetables for an irresistible vegetarian dinner!

- **Prep time: 10 minutes**
- **Cook time: 20 minutes**
- **Serves 4**

1 (15-ounce) can tomato sauce

1 (14.5-ounce) can diced tomatoes, undrained

1 cup canned full-fat coconut milk

3 garlic cloves, minced

1 small yellow onion, diced

1 teaspoon ground ginger

1 teaspoon curry powder

¾ teaspoon ground turmeric

1 tablespoon plus 1 teaspoon garam masala

1 teaspoon paprika

½ teaspoon salt (preferably pink Himalayan)

¼ teaspoon freshly ground black pepper

3 cups cooked chickpeas, drained and rinsed (about two 15-ounce cans)

2 cups hot cooked rice or quinoa

Juice of 1 lime

Cilantro, for garnish

Sliced scallions, for garnish

1. In a large saucepan, stir together the tomato sauce, diced tomatoes and their juices, coconut milk, garlic, onion, ginger, curry powder, turmeric, garam masala, paprika, salt, and pepper. Bring to a simmer over high heat. Reduce the heat to low, cover, and simmer for 20 minutes, adding the chickpeas after 10 minutes. If it starts to bubble on the sides, turn the heat down slightly.

2. Serve over the rice or quinoa and garnish with fresh lime juice, cilantro, and scallion.

VARIATION TIP: For a delicious grain-free meal, serve the chana masala over cooked spaghetti squash or cauliflower rice. Or serve in a bowl topped with steamed cauliflower or broccoli florets.

Per Serving Calories: 415; Protein: 16g; Total carbohydrates: 57g; Sugars: 15g; Fiber: 14g; Total fat: 16g; Saturated fat: 11g; Cholesterol: 0mg; Sodium: 872mg

Spaghetti Squash and Vegetable Stir-Fry

EGG-FREE, PEANUT-FREE

Stir-fry recipes are a quick and easy way to eat loads of vegetables that are packed with tons of flavor. Served on a bed of more vegetables in the form of spaghetti squash, you have a delicious grain-free meal that is bursting with the essential vitamins, minerals, and fiber the body craves. The secret to the sauce is adding a splash of oyster sauce!

- **Prep time: 20 minutes**
- **Cook time: 45 minutes**
- **Serves 4**

1 spaghetti squash

1 tablespoon extra-virgin olive oil

1½ cups vegetable broth or chicken broth

½ cup coconut aminos or gluten-free soy sauce

2 tablespoons gluten-free oyster sauce

2 tablespoons coconut sugar

2 tablespoons cornstarch

1½ tablespoons toasted sesame oil, divided

4 garlic cloves, minced

1 (2-inch) piece fresh ginger, minced (about 1 tablespoon)

1 cup baby carrots, halved lengthwise

1 cup snow peas

2 celery stalks, sliced

1 yellow onion, halved and thinly sliced

1 red bell pepper, thinly sliced

Red pepper flakes (optional)

Sesame seeds (optional)

1. Preheat the oven to 400°F.

2. Halve the spaghetti squash lengthwise and discard the seeds and strings. Brush each half with ½ tablespoon of the olive oil and place upside down in a baking pan. Add a splash of water to the bottom of the pan. Roast for 45 minutes, or until tender when pierced with a fork. Set aside until cool enough to handle. Scrape the flesh with a fork to create the noodles. Place on a serving platter and keep warm.

3. Meanwhile, in a medium bowl, whisk together the broth, coconut aminos, oyster sauce, coconut sugar, and cornstarch until blended. Set aside.

4. In a large skillet or wok, heat ½ tablespoon of sesame oil over medium heat. Add the garlic and ginger and cook for 1 minute. Scrape the garlic/ginger oil into the bowl with the sauce.

5. In the same skillet, heat the remaining 1 tablespoon of sesame oil over medium-high heat. Add the carrots, snow peas, celery, onion, and bell pepper. Cook, stirring often, for 7 minutes, or until the vegetables are tender-crisp. Add the sauce and cook for 3 minutes, stirring constantly, until thickened.

6. Spoon the vegetables and sauce over the spaghetti squash. Sprinkle with pepper flakes and sesame seeds (if using).

SIMPLIFY IT: To make the recipe more convenient, cook the squash in advance and store in the refrigerator in an airtight container for up to 3 days prior to use.

Per Serving Calories: 243; Protein: 5g; Total carbohydrates: 34g; Sugars: 11g; Fiber: 3g; Total fat: 10g; Saturated fat: 2g; Cholesterol: 0mg; Sodium: 413mg

Chicken and Bacon Carbonara

TREE NUT-FREE, PEANUT-FREE, SOY-FREE

Carbonara is hot cooked pasta tossed with a creamy blend of eggs that gives the dish a one-of-a-kind richness. I never order it out due to its high content of cream and cheese. This version is lighter, has less saturated fat, is dairy-free, and tastes absolutely delicious! The secret is to stir and toss the hot spaghetti quickly with the egg sauce. The hot pasta cooks the raw eggs, so mixing it quickly helps prevent the eggs from clumping.

- **Prep time: 20 minutes**
- **Cook time: 25 minutes**
- **Serves 8**

4 (6-ounce) boneless, skinless chicken breasts

Pinch salt (preferably pink Himalayan), plus ½ teaspoon, divided

Pinch freshly ground black pepper, plus ½ teaspoon, divided

2 tablespoons extra-virgin olive oil

2 tablespoons red wine vinegar

12 ounces bacon

1 yellow onion, chopped

3 garlic cloves, minced

1 (12-ounce) package gluten-free spaghetti

4 large eggs

1 cup unsweetened cashew milk or coconut milk beverage

½ cup nutritional yeast

¼ cup cornstarch

2 teaspoons yellow mustard

1 tablespoon chopped fresh basil

1 tablespoon chopped fresh parsley

1. Season the chicken with a pinch each of salt and pepper. In a large skillet, heat the oil and vinegar over medium-high heat. Add the chicken, cover, and cook for 4 minutes per side, or until cooked through and no longer pink. Dice the chicken and set it aside.

2. Wipe out the skillet. Set over medium-high heat, add the bacon, and cook for 8 to 12 minutes, turning frequently, until well browned. Place a paper towel on a plate and top with the cooked bacon. Place another paper towel on top and pat to absorb any extra oil. Once cooled, crumble the bacon. Set aside.

3. Pour off all but 1 tablespoon of the bacon drippings from the skillet. Set the skillet over medium heat, add the onion and garlic, and cook, stirring consistently, for 5 minutes, or until translucent.

4. In a large pot, cook the spaghetti according to package directions.

5. While the pasta is cooking, in a medium bowl, whisk together the eggs, milk, nutritional yeast, cornstarch, mustard, and ½ teaspoon each of salt and pepper.

6. Drain the spaghetti, reserving ½ cup of the pasta water. Return the spaghetti to the pot. Pour in the egg mixture and stir quickly and constantly until the sauce thickens and the eggs are cooked. Make sure to do this process quickly. If the sauce is too thick, add the reserved ½ cup pasta water.

7. Stir in the cooked chicken, bacon, and onion/garlic mixture.

Per Serving Calories: 537; Protein: 31g; Total carbohydrates: 41g; Sugars: 1g; Fiber: 2g; Total fat: 28g; Saturated fat: 8g; Cholesterol: 170mg; Sodium: 720mg

Cheesy Tomato Pasta Bake

EGG-FREE, PEANUT-FREE, SOY-FREE, VEGAN

A family-favorite dish! My mom used to make a similar recipe using canned tuna, which you can add to the recipe before baking. This is a simple meal that is kid-approved and oozing with cheese and flavor. You will never miss the dairy!

- **Prep time: 10 minutes**
- **Cook time: 35 minutes**
- **Serves 4**

8 ounces gluten-free elbow macaroni

1 (25-ounce) jar marinara sauce

2 cups shredded nondairy mozzarella cheese

¼ cup almond meal

1 tablespoon chopped fresh basil

1 tablespoon nondairy butter, melted

1. Preheat the oven 375°F. Coat a 9-by-13-inch baking dish with nonstick cooking spray.

2. In a pot of boiling water, slightly undercook the macaroni, about 3 minutes less than the package directions. Drain.

3. Spread one-third of the marinara sauce in the prepared baking dish. Top with one-third of the macaroni and one-third of the mozzarella. Repeat the layers twice. Sprinkle the top with the almond meal and basil. Drizzle with the melted butter.

4. Bake for 25 minutes, or until the top is golden brown and bubbling.

VARIATION TIP: To add protein, drain 2 cans of chicken or tuna and layer it on top of the pasta before adding the mozzarella. Or add 1 can drained and rinsed white beans.

Per Serving Calories: 477; Protein: 11g; Total carbohydrates: 64g; Sugars: 9g; Fiber: 10g; Total fat: 20g; Saturated fat: 8g; Cholesterol: 0mg; Sodium: 714mg

Barbecue Chicken and Spaghetti Squash Casserole

EGG-FREE, TREE NUT-FREE, PEANUT-FREE, SOY-FREE

This really is a tasty dish and is one of our family favorites. It is simple to make, especially if you cook the squash in advance. Using spaghetti squash in place of pasta is a great way to cut down on carbs and calories. It also absorbs lots of flavors from the barbecue sauce.

- **Prep time: 15 minutes**
- **Cook time: 1 hour**
- **Serves 4**

1 spaghetti squash

1 tablespoon extra-virgin olive oil

2 cooked chicken breasts, cut into cubes or shredded

1¼ cups Barbecue Sauce (page 165), divided

½ cup nondairy shredded mozzarella cheese, optional

¼ cup diced red onion

¼ cup diced orange bell pepper

¼ cup chopped fresh cilantro

1. Preheat the oven to 400°F.

2. Halve the spaghetti squash lengthwise and discard the seeds and strings. Brush each half with ½ tablespoon of the oil and place upside down in a baking pan. Add a splash of water to the bottom of the pan. Roast for 45 minutes, or until tender when pierced with a fork. Set aside until cool enough to handle. Scrape the flesh with a fork to release the strands.

3. Reduce the oven temperature to 350°F. Coat a 9-by-13-inch baking dish with nonstick cooking spray. Transfer the spaghetti squash to the baking dish.

4. Top with the chicken, 1 cup of barbecue sauce, the mozzarella (if using), onion, and bell pepper. Cover and bake for 15 to 20 minutes, or until hot and bubbling. Top with the remaining ¼ cup of barbecue sauce and the cilantro.

SIMPLIFY IT: This meal comes together in no time and you can have dinner on the table in 30 minutes or less by roasting the spaghetti squash in advance.

Per Serving Calories: 277; Protein: 17g; Total carbohydrates: 38g; Sugars: 21g; Fiber: 1g; Total fat: 6g; Saturated fat: 1g; Cholesterol: 44mg; Sodium: 932mg

Cold Pasta Salad with Italian Dressing

EGG-FREE, TREE NUT-FREE, PEANUT-FREE, VEGAN

Who doesn't love a classic pasta salad? This one is a favorite for kids of all ages and makes a tasty main-dish salad or side dish. It is bursting with flavor from sweet tomatoes, refreshing cucumbers, crunchy chopped broccoli, gluten-free rotini pasta, and edamame for protein. If you have the time, prepare a few hours ahead of serving time and refrigerate for the flavors to blend.

- **Prep time: 15 minutes**
- **Cook time: 10 minutes**
- **Serves 4**

1 (12-ounce) package gluten-free rotini pasta

1 large cucumber

2 cups grape tomatoes, halved

2 cups chopped broccoli

1 cup shredded carrots

1 cup shelled fresh or frozen and thawed edamame

¼ cup diced white onion

1 cup gluten-free Italian dressing, or more to taste (optional)

Freshly ground black pepper

1. Cook the rotini according to package directions. Drain and rinse under cold water to cool. Drain completely.

2. Meanwhile, peel the cucumber and halve lengthwise. Then halve lengthwise again. Cut crosswise into ¾-inch chunks.

3. In a large bowl, combine the cucumber, tomatoes, broccoli, carrots, edamame, and onion.

4. Add the pasta and 1 cup of dressing (if using) to the vegetables and toss to coat well. Add more dressing if desired. Season with pepper to taste. Serve or chill to serve later.

VARIATION TIP: This recipe is delicious with a variety of dressings. Opt for favorite gluten-free dairy-free dressings, such as balsamic vinaigrette, honey-mustard vinaigrette, or creamy Caesar—just be sure to read labels. Some safe brands include Primal Kitchen and Daiya. Or substitute Green Goddess Dressing (page 169).

Per Serving Calories: 588; Protein: 17g; Total carbohydrates: 83g; Sugars: 13g; Fiber: 12g; Total fat: 21g; Saturated fat: 4g; Cholesterol: 0mg; Sodium: 812mg

Bok Choy with Mushrooms, Red Peppers, and Noodles

EGG-FREE, PEANUT-FREE

Bok choy is a type of Chinese cabbage. Instead of growing into a head, it forms leaves similar to those of mustard greens. Look for baby bok choy, which is more tender than full-grown bok choy and delicious both raw and cooked. Sliced bok choy is mouthwatering sautéed with a bit of oil, garlic, and soy sauce until tender yet still slightly crunchy. Make sure not to overcook the vegetables, as they taste best when tender-crisp.

- **Prep time: 15 minutes**
- **Cook time: 10 minutes**
- **Serves 4**

8 ounces pad Thai rice noodles

1½ tablespoons avocado oil or vegetable oil

4 cups sliced bok choy

4 cups quartered shiitake mushroom caps

1 red bell pepper, sliced

½ tablespoon grated fresh ginger

2 garlic cloves, minced

1 cup low-sodium chicken or vegetable broth

2 tablespoons coconut aminos or gluten-free soy sauce

1 tablespoon fish sauce

½ cup diced scallion, green parts only

1 tablespoon red pepper flakes

Salt (preferably pink Himalayan)

Freshly ground black pepper

1. Cook the rice noodles according to package directions. Drain and set aside.

2. In a large skillet, heat the oil over medium-high heat. Add the bok choy, mushrooms, bell pepper, ginger, and garlic and cook, stirring constantly, for 5 to 7 minutes, or until tender-crisp.

3. Stir in the broth, coconut aminos, and fish sauce and cook, stirring, for 2 minutes, or until heated through. Add the noodles and scallion and toss to coat. Sprinkle with the pepper flakes. If desired, season with salt and black pepper to taste.

Per Serving Calories: 409; Protein: 8g; Total carbohydrates: 83g; Sugars: 8g; Fiber: 6g; Total fat: 6g; Saturated fat: 1g; Cholesterol: 0mg; Sodium: 470mg

Beef Paprikash with Fire-Roasted Tomatoes

EGG-FREE, TREE NUT-FREE, PEANUT-FREE, SOY-FREE

Hungarian beef paprikash is a stew simmered with a tomato, onion, and pepper-based broth. Created by cattle herders, it was made in the fields in cast iron kettles over open fires. The flavors here come from the vegetables, caraway seeds, and Hungarian paprika. If you can't find Hungarian paprika in stores, you can easily order it online. I like to roast the tomatoes in balsamic vinegar first to bring out a bit of natural sweetness in the fruit.

- **Prep time: 15 minutes**
- **Cook time: 2 hours**
- **Serves 4**

1 pound beef chuck, trimmed and cut into 1-inch pieces

Salt (preferably pink Himalayan)

Freshly ground black pepper

4 Campari tomatoes, halved

2 tablespoons extra-virgin olive oil, divided

1 tablespoon balsamic vinegar

1 yellow onion, minced

1 green bell pepper, diced

1 red bell pepper, diced

2 large carrots, sliced

2 garlic cloves, minced

¾ cup low-sodium beef broth

¼ cup sherry vinegar

2 tablespoons Hungarian paprika

1 teaspoon caraway seeds

¼ cup nondairy yogurt (optional)

1 (12-ounce) package gluten-free fusilli pasta

2 tablespoons chopped fresh parsley

1. Preheat the oven to 400°F.

2. Season the beef with ¼ teaspoon salt and pepper to taste and set aside.

3. Place the tomatoes in a baking pan. Drizzle with 1 tablespoon of oil and the balsamic vinegar and toss to coat. Bake for 20 to 30 minutes, or until wilted. Remove from the oven and set aside to cool. Once cooled, remove and discard the skins. In a small bowl, mash the tomatoes gently with a potato masher or spatula. Set aside.

4. Meanwhile, in a large saucepan, heat the remaining 1 tablespoon of oil over medium heat. Add the onion, bell peppers, and carrots and cook, stirring, for 5 minutes, or until browned. Add the garlic and cook for 1 minute longer.

5. Add the beef and cook for 5 minutes, stirring often, until the meat is browned.

6. Stir in the roasted tomatoes, broth, sherry vinegar, paprika, and caraway seeds. Bring to a boil. Reduce the temperature to low, cover, and simmer for about 1 hour 30 minutes. If it starts to look dry, add more water, ¼ cup at a time. If desired, season with additional salt and pepper to taste. Mix in the yogurt (if using).

7. About 15 minutes before the stew is done, cook the fusilli according to package directions. Drain.

8. Divide the fusilli and stew among four plates and garnish with the parsley.

SUBSTITUTION TIP: This hearty dish is also delish on a bed of quinoa or rice, which absorbs the flavors of the stew. For a grain-free version, serve over sautéed cauliflower rice.

Per Serving Calories: 629; Protein: 39g; Total carbohydrates: 83g; Sugars: 8g; Fiber: 6g; Total fat: 17g; Saturated fat: 4g; Cholesterol: 80mg; Sodium: 171mg

Stovetop Cheesy Pasta with Turkey Dogs and Broccoli

EGG-FREE, TREE NUT-FREE, PEANUT-FREE, SOY-FREE

Dinners just got super easy again with this one-pan meal that uses common household ingredients. Cook the pasta, then toss in the creamy ingredients, chopped hot dogs, and broccoli and you've got a wholesome dinner in minutes. It's a kid favorite (and my husband's, too!) and a healthy, delicious alternative to a boxed mac 'n' cheese mix.

- **Prep time: 5 minutes**
- **Cook time: 15 minutes**
- **Serves 4**

10 ounces gluten-free elbow macaroni or penne pasta

2 cups chopped broccoli

½ cup nutritional yeast

1 cup unsweetened cashew milk or coconut milk beverage

⅔ cup vegan mayonnaise

4 tablespoons nondairy butter

1 tablespoon Dijon mustard

½ cup cornstarch

6 turkey hot dogs, sliced into coins

Salt (preferably pink Himalayan)

Freshly ground black pepper

1. In a large pot, cook the pasta according to package directions. About 3 minutes before it's done, add the broccoli. Drain the pasta and broccoli and return to the pot.

2. Set the pot over low heat and stir in the nutritional yeast, cashew milk, mayonnaise, butter, mustard, cornstarch, and hot dogs. Stir for 5 minutes to blend the ingredients and warm the hot dogs through. If desired, season with salt and pepper to taste.

VARIATION TIP: You can easily change up this dish. Go for ham and peas, turkey and carrots, or drained tuna and cauliflower in place of the hot dogs and broccoli.

Per Serving Calories: 795; Protein: 29g; Total carbohydrates: 84g; Sugars:3 g; Fiber: 13g; Total fat: 39g; Saturated fat: 5g; Cholesterol: 52mg; Sodium: 931mg

Chinese Chicken Noodles with Peanut Dressing

EGG-FREE

The bold flavors of peanut, ginger, soy, and garlic are what make this dish spectacular. It's bursting with delicious flavors! If you want to make this dish vegetarian, skip the chicken and use drained firm tofu in its place.

- **Prep time: 10 minutes**
- **Cook time: 10 minutes**
- **Serves 4**

10 ounces pad Thai rice noodles or gluten-free spaghetti noodles

2 (6-ounce) boneless, skinless chicken breasts, thinly sliced

2 tablespoons extra-virgin olive oil, divided

2 cups bean sprouts

4 scallions, white and green parts, thinly sliced

2 garlic cloves, minced

1 carrot, thinly sliced

1 small onion, sliced

1 (1-inch) piece fresh ginger, minced

½ cup peanut butter

1 cup low-sodium chicken broth

2 tablespoons coconut aminos or gluten-free soy sauce

3 tablespoons rice vinegar

1 tablespoon oyster sauce

1 tablespoon freshly squeezed lime juice

¼ teaspoon cayenne pepper

1. Cook the rice noodles according to package directions. Drain and set aside.

2. Meanwhile, in a large skillet or wok, heat 1 tablespoon of oil over medium-high heat. Add the chicken and cook, stirring, for 3 minutes, or until browned and cooked through. Remove to a plate and set aside.

3. In the same skillet or wok, add the remaining 1 tablespoon of oil, the bean sprouts, scallions, garlic, carrot, onion, and ginger. Cook, stirring constantly, for 5 minutes, or until tender-crisp.

4. Stir in the peanut butter, broth, coconut aminos, vinegar, oyster sauce, lime juice, and cayenne and cook, stirring constantly, for 1 minute to meld the flavors. Add the noodles and chicken and toss to coat well.

SIMPLIFY IT: Prep the veggies a day or two ahead of cooking and refrigerate in an airtight container to save time. The same can be done for the sauce.

Per Serving Calories: 633; Protein: 32g; Total carbohydrates: 74g; Sugars: 8g; Fiber: 7g; Total fat: 25g; Saturated fat: 5g; Cholesterol: 49mg; Sodium: 539mg

Healthy Summer Spaghetti

EGG-FREE, TREE NUT-FREE, PEANUT-FREE, SOY-FREE

This mouthwatering pasta dish is a great way to use a bumper crop of fresh zucchini, yellow squash, and juicy tomatoes in the summer—it's so loaded with flavorful grilled vegetables, ordinary spaghetti can't compare. You can add grilled eggplant and sliced black olives for more flavor. To make the dish vegetarian, swap in 1 cup cooked cannellini beans and ½ cup chopped pecans for the chicken.

- **Prep time: 15 minutes**
- **Cook time: 30 minutes**
- **Serves 6**

2 large zucchini, trimmed

2 yellow squash, trimmed

Salt (preferably pink Himalayan)

1 white onion, trimmed

1½ tablespoons extra-virgin olive oil

1 (16-ounce) package gluten-free spaghetti

4 tomatoes, heirloom or large sweet ones

1 (32-ounce) jar marinara sauce

2 cooked chicken breasts, diced

¼ cup chopped fresh basil (optional)

1. Cut the zucchini and yellow squash lengthwise in half and then cut each in half again so you have 4 long, thin strips for each squash (a total of 16). Sprinkle the pieces with a dash of salt. Cut the onion into ½-inch rings. Set both aside.

2. Coat the grates of a grill with nonstick cooking spray. Preheat the grill to high.

3. Blot the zucchini and squash with a paper towel to remove any excess water. Place the squash and onion in a bowl and toss with the oil.

4. Reduce the grill temperature to medium-high. Arrange the vegetables on the grates and cook for 10 minutes, checking at 5 minutes to make sure they are not burning. Flip and repeat. When picking up the onions, try to keep them in their rings. Once done, remove and place on a cutting board.

5. In a large pot, cook the pasta according to package directions.

6. Meanwhile, dice the zucchini, yellow squash, and onion. Dice the tomatoes and set all aside.

7. Drain the pasta and return to the pot, add the marinara sauce, chicken, grilled vegetables, and tomatoes and toss to coat. Cook over low heat, stirring, for 2 minutes to heat through. Sprinkle with the basil (if using).

SIMPLIFY IT: Instead of grilling, you can roast the vegetables. Place them on a parchment-lined baking sheet and roast in a preheated 400°F oven for 10 minutes. Flip them and cook 10 minutes longer, or until cooked through. Adjust the temperature to broil and cook for 2 to 3 minutes, or until browned.

Per Serving Calories: 462; Protein: 28g; Total carbohydrates: 75g; Sugars: 15g; Fiber: 13g; Total fat: 6g; Saturated fat: 2g; Cholesterol: 42mg; Sodium: 783mg

Tomato, Corn, Cucumber, and Chickpea Penne Salad

EGG-FREE, TREE NUT-FREE, PEANUT-FREE, SOY-FREE, VEGAN

Enjoy the flavors of the summer with this delicious salad boasting corn, tomatoes, cucumber, and chickpeas lightly tossed with apple cider vinaigrette. Whenever you cook gluten-free pasta for a salad, make sure to not overcook it, or the pasta will be mushy and soft. Most canned beans would work in this dish, especially pinto, red kidney, or black beans.

- **Prep time: 20 minutes**
- **Cook time: 10 minutes**
- **Serves 4**

2 cups gluten-free penne pasta

2 tablespoons apple cider vinegar

1 teaspoon Dijon mustard

¼ cup extra-virgin olive oil

1 (16-ounce) bag frozen corn kernels, thawed

1 (15-ounce) can chickpeas, drained and rinsed

1 cup grape tomatoes, halved

1 cucumber, peeled, quartered lengthwise, and sliced

⅓ cup diced scallions, white and green parts

Salt (preferably pink Himalayan)

Freshly ground black pepper

1. Cook the noodles according to package directions. Rinse under cold running water and drain.

2. In a large bowl, whisk together the vinegar and mustard. Whisk in the oil until well blended. Add the corn, chickpeas, tomatoes, cucumber, scallions, and drained pasta and toss to coat well. If desired, season with salt and pepper to taste.

3. Serve room temperature or refrigerate to serve later.

Per Serving Calories: 436; Protein: 12g; Total carbohydrates: 67g; Sugars: 9g; Fiber: 9g; Total fat: 16g; Saturated fat: 2g; Cholesterol: 0mg; Sodium: 48mg

Seafood

Halibut with Mango Salsa Verde, page 90

Shrimp and Scallop Pasta in Cajun Garlic Cream Sauce

EGG-FREE, TREE NUT-FREE, PEANUT-FREE, SOY-FREE

This rich and creamy meal is a favorite in our house! A special dish that tastes like it's from a French Quarter restaurant in New Orleans but is simple enough for any cook. If you are new to Cajun seasoning, start with 1 tablespoon and taste the sauce, adding up to 2 tablespoons for a super-spicy dish.

- **Prep time: 10 minutes**
- **Cook time: 30 minutes**
- **Serves 6**

2 tablespoons extra-virgin olive oil, divided

1 cup diced white onion

1 red bell pepper, sliced

1 green bell pepper, sliced

1 pound peeled and deveined jumbo shrimp or king prawns

1 pound scallops

2 garlic cloves, minced

8 ounces nondairy cream cheese

1 cup white wine

½ cup unsweetened cashew milk or coconut milk beverage

2 tablespoons tomato paste

1 vegetable bouillon cube (no salt added)

1 to 2 tablespoons Cajun seasoning

½ teaspoon salt (preferably pink Himalayan)

¼ teaspoon freshly ground black pepper

1 (16-ounce) package gluten-free fusilli pasta

1 tablespoon chopped fresh parsley (optional)

1. In a large skillet, heat 1 tablespoon of oil over medium-high heat. Add the onion and bell peppers. Cook, stirring often, for 10 minutes, or until the onions become translucent. Transfer to a bowl and set aside.

2. In the same skillet, heat the remaining 1 tablespoon of oil over medium-high heat. Add the shrimp and scallops and cook without stirring for 2 minutes, or until they're lightly browned and don't stick to the pan. Flip and cook for 2 to 3 minutes longer, or until the shrimp turns pink and the scallops are opaque. Make sure not to overcook them. Transfer to a cutting board and set aside to cool. When cool enough to handle, cut both into thirds. Place in the bowl with the onion-pepper mixture.

3. In the same skillet, cook the garlic over medium heat for 1 minute. Add the cream cheese, wine, milk, tomato paste, bouillon cube, Cajun seasoning, salt, and black pepper. Cook, whisking constantly, until the cheese melts and the bouillon dissolves. Cover and cook over low heat for 15 minutes to blend the flavors.

4. Meanwhile, cook the pasta according to package directions. Drain, reserving ¼ cup of the water.

5. Add the drained pasta to the skillet with the vegetable seafood mixture and toss to coat well. Cook for 2 minutes on low heat or until heated through, adding some of the pasta water to thin the sauce if needed. Garnish with chopped parsley (if using).

Per Serving Calories: 648; Protein: 42g; Total carbohydrates: 73g; Sugars: 5g; Fiber: 3g; Total fat: 18g; Saturated fat: 4g; Cholesterol: 176mg; Sodium: 1,051mg

Teriyaki Salmon with Garlic Butter Asparagus

EGG-FREE, PEANUT-FREE

This delicious salmon is marinated in homemade teriyaki sauce, then pan-fried to seal in the flavors before roasting to create a perfectly crisp crust. Enjoy it with garlicky asparagus along with steamed rice, roasted potatoes, freshly cooked quinoa, or gluten-free pasta.

- **Prep time: 15 minutes, plus 30 minutes to marinate**
- **Cook time: 20 minutes**
- **Serves 4**

FOR THE SALMON

⅓ cup mirin (Japanese sweet rice wine)

½ cup gluten-free soy sauce or coconut aminos

2 tablespoons coconut sugar

2 tablespoons freshly squeezed lime juice

2 teaspoons toasted sesame oil

3 garlic cloves, minced

1 (1-inch) piece fresh ginger, minced

4 (6-ounce) skin-on salmon fillets (preferably wild-caught)

2 tablespoons nondairy butter

FOR THE ASPARAGUS

2 tablespoons nondairy butter

2 garlic cloves, minced

1 pound asparagus, trimmed

1 teaspoon grated lemon zest

Salt (preferably pink Himalayan)

Freshly ground black pepper

TO MAKE THE SALMON

1. In a 9-by-13-inch baking dish, whisk together the mirin, soy sauce, coconut sugar, lime juice, oil, garlic, and ginger. Place the salmon skin-side up in the sauce. Cover and refrigerate for at least 30 minutes but no longer than 1 hour.

2. Preheat the oven to 425°F.

3. In a large ovenproof skillet, heat the butter over medium-high heat. Swirl the butter to coat the skillet. Remove the salmon from the marinade, reserving the marinade. Place the salmon in the skillet, skin-side up. Cook for 2 minutes. Flip the salmon and spoon ½ cup of the marinade on top. Place the skillet in the oven and roast for 8 minutes, or until browned and the fish is opaque.

In a skillet over medium heat, melt the butter. Add the garlic and cook, stirring, for 1 minute. Add the asparagus and cook, turning often, for 8 minutes, or until tender-crisp. Sprinkle with the lemon zest. If desired, add salt and pepper to taste. Serve with the salmon.

INGREDIENT TIP: Wild salmon is preferable to farm-raised salmon, which is usually fed antibiotics to prevent disease in the farm tanks. Sometimes you can find wild-caught salmon at a good price in the frozen foods section. If using frozen salmon, make sure to let it thaw completely before using.

Per Serving Calories: 443; Protein: 45g; Total carbohydrates: 19g; Sugars: 9g; Fiber: 3g; Total fat: 21g; Saturated fat: 4g; Cholesterol: 60mg; Sodium: 545mg

Tuna Salad Stuffed Tomatoes

EGG-FREE, TREE NUT-FREE, PEANUT-FREE, SOY-FREE

Tuna salads were a staple lunch item in my home growing up. My mom made them often, and I loved sinking my teeth into the creamy seafood with little crunches of celery. Whenever we would go out to lunch, she'd order a tuna-stuffed tomato if it was on the menu. I love making it at home so I can control the amount of mayo—feel free to add more or less depending on your preference.

- **Prep time: 20 minutes**
- **Serves 4**

4 large beefsteak tomatoes

2 (5-ounce) cans albacore tuna in water, drained

½ cup finely diced celery

⅓ cup vegan mayonnaise

¼ cup minced onion

1 tablespoon yellow mustard

1 tablespoon chopped fresh dill, plus more for garnish

2 teaspoons freshly squeezed lemon juice

¼ teaspoon salt (preferably pink Himalayan)

¼ teaspoon ground white pepper

Paprika, for garnish

1. Slice the tops off the tomatoes and reserve. With a spoon, scoop out the insides and the seeds, like you would when carving a pumpkin. Set aside.

2. In a medium bowl, combine the tuna, celery, mayonnaise, onion, mustard, dill, lemon juice, salt, and pepper.

3. Spoon the tuna mixture into the tomatoes, dividing evenly. Garnish with extra dill and a sprinkle of paprika. Set the reserved tomato tops on top like little hats.

Per Serving Calories: 172; Protein: 20 g; Total carbohydrates: 10g; Sugars: 5g; Fiber: 3g; Total fat: 6g; Saturated fat: 0g; Cholesterol: 21mg; Sodium: 395mg

Herb-Pecan Rubbed Salmon

EGG-FREE, PEANUT-FREE, SOY-FREE

This recipe is inspired by my mom and sister's Christmas adventure in Aspen. They took a carriage ride to a quaint little restaurant where they ordered the most magnificent maple and pecan crusted salmon. This version has sweet and nutty flavors that complement the herbs infused into this special seafood rub. The complex flavors are quite simple to prepare. Enjoy with a side of roasted vegetables or Garlic Butter Asparagus (from Teriyaki Salmon, page 78).

- **Prep time: 10 minutes**
- **Cook time: 10 minutes**
- **Serves 4**

1 cup pecans

1 handful fresh dill

1 handful fresh cilantro, stems included

2 tablespoons extra-virgin olive oil

2 tablespoons fresh lemon juice

2 tablespoons maple syrup

½ teaspoon salt

½ teaspoon freshly ground black pepper

4 (6-ounce) salmon fillets (preferably wild-caught), skinned

2 tablespoons nondairy butter

1. Preheat the oven to 425°F.

2. In a food processor, combine the pecans, dill, cilantro, oil, lemon juice, maple syrup, salt, and pepper. Pulse to achieve a fine crumb.

3. Generously season both sides of the salmon with the mixture.

4. In a large ovenproof skillet, heat the butter over medium-high heat. Swirl the butter to coat the skillet. Place the salmon in the skillet, skin-side up. Cook for 2 minutes. Flip the salmon, place the skillet in the oven, and roast for 8 minutes, or until browned and the fish is opaque.

VARIATION TIP: To make this nut-free, skip the pecan coating (although that is what gives this dish depth). Instead, mix ¾ cup vegan mayonnaise with the herbs (omit the maple syrup and olive oil) to turn it into a creamy herb sauce to dollop on top of the fish, for serving.

Per Serving Calories: 567; Protein: 45g; Total carbohydrates: 11g; Sugars: 7g; Fiber: 3g; Total fat: 40g; Saturated fat: 6g; Cholesterol: 60mg; Sodium: 621mg

Tuna Salad Avocado Boats

EGG-FREE, TREE NUT-FREE, PEANUT-FREE, SOY-FREE

A light and energizing lunch that is packed full of healthy omega-3s (brain fuel) and muscle-building protein. It makes a nice lunch or light dinner for last-minute guests, so if you (or they) are looking for an easy, tasty, low-carb dish, this one is your golden ticket!

- **Prep time: 15 minutes**
- **Serves 4**

2 (5-ounce) cans albacore tuna packed in water, drained

½ cup diced celery

½ finely diced red bell pepper

⅓ cup vegan mayonnaise

⅓ cup chopped scallion greens

1 tablespoon chopped fresh cilantro, plus more for garnish

1 tablespoon yellow mustard

2 teaspoons freshly squeezed lemon juice

¼ teaspoon salt (preferably pink Himalayan)

¼ teaspoon ground white pepper

4 large avocados

Chili powder, for garnish

1. In a medium bowl, combine the tuna, celery, bell pepper, mayonnaise, scallion, cilantro, mustard, lemon juice, salt, and pepper.

2. Halve and pit the avocados. Evenly divide the tuna mixture into the avocado halves. Garnish with cilantro and a sprinkle of chili powder.

VARIATION TIP: To change it up, you can use canned crabmeat or canned chicken in place of tuna.

Per Serving Calories: 544; Protein: 23g; Total carbohydrates: 21g; Sugars: 2g; Fiber: 16g; Total fat: 44g; Saturated fat: 5g; Cholesterol: 30mg; Sodium: 626mg

Blackened Rockfish with Avocado Mango Salsa

EGG-FREE, TREE NUT-FREE, PEANUT-FREE, SOY-FREE

This tender white fish is baked in the best blackened seasoning recipe and dressed with a sweet and crunchy salsa. This rockfish recipe will rock your world! This dish goes great over a salad or vegetables, or in a fish taco.

- **Prep time: 15 minutes**
- **Cook time: 10 minutes**
- **Serves 4**

FOR THE SALSA

2 large avocados (not overly ripe), diced

1 mango, diced

¼ cup diced red onion

¼ cup chopped fresh cilantro

Juice of ½ lime

½ teaspoon salt (preferably pink Himalayan)

FOR THE ROCKFISH

1 tablespoon smoked paprika (or regular)

2 teaspoons coconut sugar

1 teaspoon cayenne pepper

½ teaspoon garlic powder

½ teaspoon dried thyme

½ teaspoon dried oregano

½ teaspoon dried basil

½ teaspoon salt (preferably pink Himalayan)

½ teaspoon freshly ground black pepper

1½ tablespoons extra-virgin olive oil

4 (6-ounce) rockfish, red snapper, or cod fillets

TO MAKE THE SALSA

In a medium bowl, combine the avocado, mango, onion, cilantro, lime juice, and salt and gently toss to blend. Set aside.

TO MAKE THE ROCKFISH

1. In a small bowl, stir together the paprika, coconut sugar, cayenne, garlic powder, thyme, oregano, basil, salt, and pepper. Set aside.

2. Preheat the oven to broil with a rack 6 inches from the heat.

3. Drizzle the oil into a 9-by-13-inch baking dish. Add the fish to the baking dish, sprinkle with the seasoning mix, and rub the seasoning into the fish, including the sides and bottom.

4. Broil for 6 to 10 minutes, flipping once, or until the fish flakes when tested with a fork. If it starts to burn on top, cover with aluminum foil. Serve with the salsa.

Per Serving Calories: 393; Protein: 33g; Total carbohydrates: 25g; Sugars: 15g; Fiber: 8g; Total fat: 21g; Saturated fat: 3g; Cholesterol: 83mg; Sodium: 584mg

Cauliflower, Broccoli, and Shrimp Tart

EGG-FREE, PEANUT-FREE, SOY-FREE

Tarts are perfect to serve at a brunch, lunch, or for dinner. This one has a creaminess reminiscent of a dairy-filled tart. It's a complete balanced meal filled with vegetables and proteins baked into a soft, flaky, buttery herb crust. To make this dish vegan, skip the shrimp and incorporate ½ cup more cauliflower.

- **Prep time: 20 minutes**
- **Cook time: 45 minutes**
- **Serves 8**

FOR THE CRUST

1 cup all-purpose gluten-free flour, plus more for dusting

¼ cup almond meal

1 teaspoon dried dill

½ teaspoon dried tarragon

¼ teaspoon salt (preferably pink Himalayan)

6 tablespoons cold water

4 tablespoons nondairy butter

FOR THE FILLING

4 tablespoons nondairy butter

¾ cup finely diced yellow onion

½ cup finely diced cauliflower florets

½ cup finely diced broccoli florets

1 tablespoon all-purpose gluten-free flour

½ cup vegetable broth

1⅓ cups shredded nondairy mozzarella cheese, divided

1 (5-ounce) can baby shrimp, drained

Salt (preferably pink Himalayan)

Freshly ground black pepper

Paprika, for garnish

TO MAKE THE CRUST

1. In a medium bowl, stir together the flour, almond meal, dill, tarragon, salt, and water. With a pastry blender or two knives, cut in the butter until crumbs form. Using your hands or a spatula, form into a dough.

2. Preheat the oven to 375°F. Coat a 9-inch round tart pan with nonstick cooking spray.

3. On a lightly floured piece of parchment paper, roll the dough into a 10-inch round. Flip the parchment paper over the tart pan, reserving the paper. Press the dough into the pan so it evenly covers the bottom and sides of the pan.

4. Prick the bottom of the dough with a fork a few times and cover with the parchment paper. Bake for 15 minutes. Remove the parchment paper and bake for 5 minutes longer, or until lightly browned.

1. In a large skillet, melt the butter over medium-high heat. Add the onion, cauliflower, and broccoli and cook, stirring often, for 5 minutes, or until tender. Add the flour and cook, stirring, for 1 minute. Stir in the broth and bring to a boil, then remove from the heat. Add 1 cup of mozzarella and the shrimp and stir until the cheese melts. If desired, season with salt and pepper to taste.

2. Spoon the cheese mixture into the tart shell. Sprinkle with the remaining ⅓ cup of mozzarella and bake for 10 minutes, or until hot and bubbling. Garnish with paprika. Let stand for 5 minutes before cutting into 8 wedges.

Per Serving Calories: 311; Protein: 8g; Total carbohydrates: 23g; Sugars: 2g; Fiber: 5g; Total fat: 25g; Saturated fat: 3g; Cholesterol: 45mg; Sodium: 309mg

Grilled Bacon-Wrapped Shrimp

EGG-FREE, TREE NUT-FREE, PEANUT-FREE, SOY-FREE

This recipe is delectable as an appetizer or part of a main dish. You can serve the shrimp on skewers, over rice, or over one of the salads in this book. If using as the protein in a main dish, allow five shrimp per serving. Enjoy these flavorful bites as your go-to for summer barbecues, cocktail parties, or lunches in the garden.

- **Prep time: 25 minutes, plus 30 minutes to marinate**
- **Cook time: 10 minutes**
- **Makes 20 shrimp**

1 tablespoon maple syrup

1 tablespoon extra-virgin olive oil

2 teaspoons apple cider vinegar

1 teaspoon paprika

½ teaspoon ground cumin

½ teaspoon garlic salt

½ teaspoon freshly ground black pepper

20 jumbo shrimp, peeled and deveined

10 bacon slices, halved crosswise

Juice of 1 lemon, for serving

Paprika, for serving

1. In a medium bowl, stir together the maple syrup, oil, vinegar, paprika, cumin, garlic salt, and pepper. Rinse the shrimp and pat dry with a paper towel. Add the shrimp to the bowl. Cover and marinate in the refrigerator for at least 30 minutes but not more than 1 hour.

2. Meanwhile, in a large skillet, cook the bacon over medium heat for 2 minutes, just until the sides start to brown but are not cooked. Place a paper towel on a plate and top with the cooked bacon. Place another paper towel on top and pat to absorb any extra oil.

3. Working with one shrimp at a time, remove from the marinade and wrap with a slice of bacon. Fasten it with a toothpick. Reserve the marinade.

4. Preheat the grill to medium.

5. Place the shrimp on the grill grates (or in a grill basket) and brush with some of the marinade. Grill for 4 minutes. Brush again with the marinade and flip the shrimp. Grill for 4 to 6 minutes longer, or until the shrimp are opaque. Serve immediately with a splash of fresh lemon juice and sprinkle of paprika.

INGREDIENT TIP: Make sure not to overcook the shrimp, as that will make them tough and chewy. Cooking the bacon in advance helps ensure the shrimp is tender and the bacon isn't undercooked.

Per Serving Calories: 44; Protein: 5g; Total carbohydrates: 1g; Sugars: 1g; Fiber <1g; Total fat: 3g; Saturated fat: 1g; Cholesterol: 28mg; Sodium: 148mg

Salmon Cakes with Spicy Aioli

TREE NUT-FREE, PEANUT-FREE, SOY-FREE

These savory fish cakes are baked and broiled to crispy perfection! Crab cakes and salmon cakes are a favorite dish that can be easily made at home in as little as 45 minutes. Serve with this spicy yogurt dipping sauce and your guests will be talking about it for years to come.

- **Prep time: 15 minutes**
- **Cook time: 30 minutes**
- **Serves 4**

FOR THE SALMON CAKES

1 large egg

1 tablespoon vegan mayonnaise

1 teaspoon freshly squeezed lemon juice

2 (5-ounce) cans salmon, without bones

½ cup gluten-free bread crumbs, such as panko

¼ cup finely diced onion

¼ cup finely diced red bell pepper

1 teaspoon Old Bay seasoning

½ teaspoon dried parsley

½ teaspoon mustard powder

½ teaspoon baking powder

1 tablespoon chopped fresh chives or 1 teaspoon dried

⅛ teaspoon cayenne pepper (optional)

Salt (preferably pink Himalayan)

Freshly ground black pepper

FOR THE AIOLI

½ cup nondairy yogurt

2 teaspoons honey

1 teaspoon freshly squeezed lime juice

1 teaspoon distilled white vinegar

½ teaspoon chili powder

½ teaspoon paprika

¼ teaspoon ground cumin

¼ teaspoon garlic powder

¼ teaspoon salt

¼ teaspoon dried oregano

1 tablespoon nondairy butter, melted

TO MAKE THE SALMON CAKES

1. Preheat the oven to 375°F. Line a baking sheet with parchment paper.

2. In a medium bowl, whisk together the egg, mayonnaise, and lemon juice. Add the salmon, bread crumbs, onion, bell pepper, Old Bay, parsley, mustard powder, baking powder, chives, cayenne (if using), and salt and black pepper to taste. Gently stir until well blended, breaking up any chunks of salmon as you stir.

3. With a spatula, divide the mixture into four portions. With your hands, form each portion into a patty and place on the prepared baking sheet.

4. Bake for 15 minutes. Flip the salmon cakes and bake for 10 minutes longer.

TO MAKE THE AIOLI

1. In a small bowl, whisk together the yogurt, honey, lime juice, vinegar, chili powder, paprika, cumin, garlic powder, salt, and oregano. Stir in the melted butter. Refrigerate until ready to use.

2. Preheat the broiler and broil the cakes for 3 to 5 minutes, or until the tops are lightly browned. Serve with the spicy aioli.

VARIATION TIP: You can swap out the salmon in this mouthwatering fish cake recipe for canned crab or tuna.

Per Serving Calories: 230; Protein: 18g; Total carbohydrates: 16g; Sugars: 5g; Fiber: 1g; Total fat: 10g; Saturated fat: 2g; Cholesterol: 68mg; Sodium: 513mg

Halibut with Mango Salsa Verde

EGG-FREE, PEANUT-FREE, SOY-FREE

What I love about this summer dish is the fresh mango. These sweet and juicy fruits pair well with green tomatillos. Although they look similar to tomatoes, tomatillos are unrelated and have a subtle citrus-like flavor. Tomatillos are a favorite ingredient of mine for salsa or as a topping for meats. Remove the husks of the tomatillos and rinse before chopping.

- **Prep time: 10 minutes, plus 1 hour to marinate**
- **Cook time: 10 minutes**
- **Serves 4**

FOR THE HALIBUT

4 tomatillos, diced

¼ cup chopped fresh cilantro

¼ diced red onion

2 garlic cloves, minced

1 tablespoon freshly squeezed lime juice

½ teaspoon salt, (preferably pink Himalayan)

¼ teaspoon freshly ground black pepper

4 (6-ounce) halibut, flounder, or cod fillets

FOR THE SALSA

4 tomatillos, diced

1 cup diced mango

¼ cup finely diced red onion

¼ cup chopped fresh cilantro

¼ cup chopped walnuts

1 tablespoon chopped fresh mint

1 tablespoon freshly squeezed lime juice

¼ teaspoon salt (preferably pink Himalayan)

TO MAKE THE HALIBUT

In a large baking dish or large zip-top bag, combine the tomatillos, cilantro, onion, garlic, lime juice, salt, and pepper. Rinse the halibut under cold water and pat it dry with a paper towel. Add the fish to the marinade, turning to coat. Cover and marinate in the refrigerator for 1 hour.

TO MAKE THE SALSA

1. In a medium bowl, combine the tomatillos, mango, onion, cilantro, walnuts, mint, lime juice, and salt. Cover and refrigerate until ready to use.

2. Position a rack 6 to 8 inches from the heat and preheat the broiler.

3. Broil the fish for 6 to 8 minutes, flipping once, or until the fish flakes easily with a fork. Serve topped with the salsa.

RECIPE TIP: Make the salsa the same day for the best texture.

Per Serving Calories: 281; Protein: 38g; Total carbohydrates: 14g; Sugars: 7g; Fiber: 3g; Total fat: 9g; Saturated fat: 1g; Cholesterol: 55mg; Sodium: 386mg

Poultry

Creamy Tuscan Sun-Dried Tomato Chicken, page 100

"Fried" Chicken Cutlets

TREE NUT-FREE, PEANUT-FREE, SOY-FREE

This "fried" chicken is healthier (and faster) than traditional because it's baked instead of fried. When I was growing up in southern Virginia, my mom always made fried chicken cutlets for dinner. She would prepare a large batch and freeze what we didn't eat for another night. Double this recipe and do what my mother did: Freeze the leftovers in a sealed zip-top bag with the air removed. They'll keep for up to 3 months.

- **Prep time: 10 minutes**
- **Cook time: 20 minutes**
- **Serves 4**

3 tablespoons extra-virgin olive oil, divided

4 (6-ounce) boneless, skinless chicken breasts

2 large eggs

1¼ cups all-purpose gluten-free flour

1 tablespoon salt-free lemon-pepper seasoning

1 teaspoon paprika

1 teaspoon salt (preferably pink Himalayan)

1. Preheat the oven to 400°F. Brush a rimmed baking sheet with 1½ tablespoons of oil.

2. Place a chicken breast on a cutting board and slice in half horizontally to make 2 cutlets. Using a meat mallet, pound the cutlets to tenderize and flatten. Repeat for a total of 8 cutlets.

3. In a small bowl, whisk together the eggs. In a pie dish or a shallow baking dish, stir together the flour, lemon-pepper seasoning, paprika, and salt.

4. Working with one cutlet at a time, dip into the flour mixture, then the egg, and then back in the flour. Place the chicken on the prepared baking sheet. Drizzle all the cutlets with the remaining 1½ tablespoons of oil.

5. Bake for 20 minutes, or until the chicken is cooked through.

VARIATION TIP: The oil-drizzled breading makes this chicken crisp yet tender, but if you'd like to make it grain-free, use almond meal in place of flour.

Per Serving Calories: 418; Protein: 42g; Total carbohydrates: 28g; Sugars: <1g; Fiber: 1g; Total fat: 17g; Saturated fat: 3g; Cholesterol: 191mg; Sodium: 887mg

Chicken Fried Rice

PEANUT-FREE, SOY-FREE

Fried rice is an all-time favorite and is simple to make at home. Using canned chicken makes this meal even easier. Rice vinegar, sesame oil, and coconut aminos impart abundant flavors when tossed with rice, eggs, carrots, peas, and onion. Enjoy it as a side dish for four people or serve it as a main dish for two people.

- **Prep time: 10 minutes**
- **Cook time: 20 minutes**
- **Serves 2**

1½ cups long-grain white rice

2 teaspoons avocado oil or vegetable oil, divided

2 large eggs

1 (5-ounce) can chicken

⅓ cup finely diced onion

1 carrot, finely diced

½ cup frozen peas, thawed

1½ tablespoons coconut aminos or gluten-free soy sauce

2 teaspoons rice vinegar

1½ teaspoons toasted sesame oil

Salt (preferably pink Himalayan)

Freshly ground black pepper

1. In a small saucepan, cook the rice according to package directions.

2. Meanwhile, in a large skillet, heat 1 teaspoon of avocado oil over medium-high heat. Add the eggs and cook, stirring constantly, for 2 minutes, or until the eggs are cooked through. Remove from the heat, transfer to a bowl, and set aside.

3. In the same skillet, heat the remaining 1 teaspoon of avocado oil over medium-high heat. Add the chicken, onion, carrot, peas, coconut aminos, and vinegar. Cook for 3 minutes, stirring often, to heat through.

4. Remove from the heat and stir in the rice, cooked eggs, and sesame oil. If desired, season with salt and pepper to taste.

VARIATION TIP: This basic recipe can easily be changed up for variety. Substitute brown rice for the white, just remember it takes 45 minutes to cook instead of 20, or use leftover rice. Swap out the canned chicken for drained canned shrimp or salmon, or use ¾ cup of diced cooked chicken.

Per Serving Calories: 821; Protein: 39g; Total carbohydrates: 123g; Sugars: 5g; Fiber: 5g; Total fat: 16g; Saturated fat: 3g; Cholesterol: 191mg; Sodium: 183mg

Chicken Cacciatore

EGG-FREE, TREE NUT-FREE, PEANUT-FREE, SOY-FREE

For years, this has always been one of my favorite healthy chicken dishes that I order anytime I'm at an Italian restaurant. It's packed with protein and vegetables, making it a lovely low-carb meal. Enjoy it by itself, over noodles or spaghetti squash, or served with a side salad.

- **Prep time: 10 minutes**
- **Cook time: 30 minutes**
- **Serves 4**

4 (6-ounce) boneless, skinless chicken breasts

⅓ cup all-purpose gluten-free flour

1½ tablespoons Italian seasoning, divided

½ teaspoon salt (preferably pink Himalayan)

½ teaspoon freshly ground black pepper

¼ cup extra-virgin olive oil

1½ cups sliced mushrooms

1 green bell pepper, diced

1 red bell pepper, diced

1 garlic clove, minced

2 cups canned tomato sauce

½ cup chicken broth

¼ cup dry white wine

1 tablespoon chopped fresh parsley, for garnish

1. Place the chicken on a cutting board and, using a meat mallet, pound the chicken to tenderize and flatten slightly. In a zip-top bag, add the flour, 1 tablespoon of Italian seasoning, the salt, and pepper. Add the chicken, seal the bag, and toss until the chicken is coated.

2. In a large skillet, heat the oil over medium-high heat. Add the chicken and cook for 2 minutes per side, turning once, until browned. Remove the chicken to a plate.

3. In the same skillet, add the mushrooms, bell peppers, and garlic. Cook over medium-high heat for 5 minutes, or until soft. Add the remaining ½ tablespoon of Italian seasoning, the tomato sauce, broth, and wine. Bring to a boil and cook for 5 minutes, then reduce to a simmer.

4. Return the chicken to the pan, cover, and simmer for 10 minutes to blend the flavors. Uncover and cook about 5 minutes longer, or until the liquid begins to thicken and a thermometer inserted in the thickest part of the chicken reaches 165°F.

5. Transfer to a serving plate and garnish with parsley.

RECIPE TIP: Choose a good dry white wine that is delicious enough to drink. If you wouldn't drink it, do not use it to add flavor to the dish. If it tastes good on the lips, it brings out delicate flavor in this sauce.

Per Serving Calories: 397; Protein: 39g; Total carbohydrates: 23g; Sugars: 7g; Figer: 5g; Total fat: 18g; Saturated fat: 3g; Cholesterol: 98mg; Sodium: 1,278mg

Italian Chicken with Pesto Fingerling Potatoes

EGG-FREE, PEANUT-FREE, SOY-FREE

This chicken is cooked to a perfect crispy exterior and seasoned with Italian flavors and zesty lemon juice. Using fingerling potatoes keeps the side simple and the chopping at a minimum since they are long, thin, and small.

- **Prep time: 5 minutes**
- **Cook time: 25 minutes**
- **Serves 4**

FOR THE CHICKEN

4 tablespoons nondairy butter, melted

3 tablespoons freshly squeezed lemon juice

1½ tablespoons Italian seasoning

4 (6-ounce) boneless, skinless chicken breasts

Salt (preferably pink Himalayan)

Freshly ground black pepper

FOR THE PESTO POTATOES

Salt (preferably pink Himalayan)

1 pound small fingerling potatoes

1 cup fresh basil leaves

2 tablespoons pine nuts

2 garlic cloves

1 teaspoon nutritional yeast

Salt (preferably pink Himalayan)

¼ teaspoon freshly ground black pepper

⅓ cup extra-virgin olive oil

TO MAKE THE CHICKEN

1. Preheat the oven to broil.

2. In a 9-inch baking dish, stir together the melted butter, lemon juice, and Italian seasoning. Dip the chicken in the mixture and flip to coat both sides. Season with a dash of salt and pepper.

3. Broil the chicken for 5 minutes per side, turning once. Reduce the temperature to 350°F and bake the chicken for 15 minutes, or until a thermometer inserted in the thickest part of the chicken reaches 165°F.

TO MAKE THE PESTO POTATOES

1. Bring a saucepan of salted water to a boil over high heat. Add the potatoes, reduce the heat to medium-low, and simmer for 15 minutes, or until the potatoes are tender. Drain and transfer to a serving bowl.

2. While the potatoes cook, in a food processor, combine the basil, pine nuts, garlic, nutritional yeast, pepper, and ¼ teaspoon salt. Process for 30 seconds, adding the oil gradually until smooth.

3. Spoon the pesto sauce over the potatoes and mix well. Serve the chicken with the pesto potatoes.

SIMPLIFY IT: Make the pesto up to 2 days in advance. Let it come to room temperature to liquefy the oil before adding it to the potatoes. You can even add a dollop on top of the cooked chicken.

Per Serving Calories: 544; Protein: 38g; Total carbohydrates: 21g; Sugars: 1g; Fiber: 4g; Total fat: 36g; Saturated fat: 7g; Cholesterol: 98mg; Sodium: 412mg

Creamy Tuscan Sun-Dried Tomato Chicken

EGG-FREE, TREE NUT-FREE, PEANUT-FREE, SOY-FREE

This healthy Tuscan-inspired creamy sauce is bursting with flavor from sweet sun-dried tomatoes, earthy mushrooms, fresh basil, and garlic and is a delectable coating for pan-seared chicken. Reminiscent of a high-end restaurant entrée, this easy meal is ready in just 40 minutes, and simple enough for weeknights but elegant enough for company.

- **Prep time: 10 minutes**
- **Cook time: 30 minutes**
- **Serves 4**

2 tablespoons nondairy butter

4 (6-ounce) boneless, skinless chicken breasts

8 ounces mushrooms, sliced

3 garlic cloves, minced

1 cup vegetable broth

⅓ cup white wine

½ teaspoon salt (preferably pink Himalayan)

¼ teaspoon freshly ground black pepper

1 cup nondairy yogurt

1 tablespoon cornstarch

1 cup sun-dried tomatoes in olive oil, drained with oil reserved, chopped

3 cups baby spinach

2 tablespoons chopped fresh basil

1. Preheat the oven 400°F.

2. In a large skillet, heat the butter over medium-high heat. Add the chicken and cook for 4 minutes per side, turning once. Transfer the chicken to a baking dish and bake in the oven for 15 minutes.

3. Meanwhile, in the same skillet, cook the mushrooms over medium heat, stirring, for 5 minutes, or until browned. Add the garlic and cook, stirring, for 1 minute. Stir in the broth, wine, salt, and pepper.

4. When the chicken comes out of the oven, return it to the skillet and simmer over medium heat for 5 minutes, or until a thermometer inserted in the thickest part of the chicken reaches 165°F.

5. In a small bowl, stir together the yogurt and cornstarch. Whisk into the skillet. Add the sun-dried tomatoes, spinach, and basil and cook, stirring, for 3 minutes, or until the sauce thickens and the spinach wilts.

RECIPE TIP: This dish is so versatile it can be served over a bed of pasta or rice, with a side of roasted or steamed potatoes, or with a side salad or steamed broccoli for a lower-carb meal.

Per Serving Calories: 449; Protein: 41g; Total carbohydrates: 20g; Sugars: 8g; Fiber: 4g; Total fat: 23g; Saturated fat: 4g; Cholesterol: 98mg; Sodium: 1,331mg

Spicy Grilled Chicken, Avocado, and Tomato Sandwich

EGG-FREE, TREE NUT-FREE, PEANUT-FREE, SOY-FREE

One of our favorite places to dine is a local pizza place that makes a divine sandwich that's my husband's go-to order and the inspiration for this recipe. It's bursting with Southwestern flavors and makes the perfect summer lunch or light dinner served with vegetable sticks or gluten-free chips and fresh lemonade.

- **Prep time: 15 minutes, plus 1 hour to marinate**
- **Cook time: 15 minutes**
- **Serves 4**

1 tablespoon extra-virgin olive oil

1 tablespoon freshly squeezed lime juice, plus 2 teaspoons, divided

1 garlic clove, minced

¼ teaspoon salt (preferably pink Himalayan)

¼ teaspoon freshly ground black pepper

¼ teaspoon cayenne pepper

1 jalapeño pepper, seeded and diced

2 (6-ounce) boneless, skinless chicken breasts

4 tablespoons nondairy yogurt

¼ teaspoon ground coriander

¼ teaspoon chili powder

8 slices gluten-free bread

1 avocado, sliced

1 beefsteak tomato, sliced

8 to 12 butter lettuce leaves

1. In a zip-top bag, combine the oil, 1 tablespoon of lime juice, the garlic, salt, black pepper, cayenne, and jalapeño. Add the chicken and close tightly, removing extra air. Place in the refrigerator to marinate for at least 1 hour or up to overnight.

2. Meanwhile, in a small bowl, stir together the yogurt, remaining 2 teaspoons of lime juice, coriander, and chili powder. Cover and refrigerate until ready to use.

3. Preheat the grill to medium.

4. Remove the chicken from the marinade. Grill for 12 to 15 minutes, flipping every 4 minutes, until browned and a thermometer inserted in the thickest part of the chicken reaches 165°F. Slice the chicken into thin strips.

5. Place 1 slice of bread on each of four plates. Evenly divide the avocado, chicken, tomato, yogurt mixture, and lettuce among the bread slices. Top with the remaining slices of bread.

RECIPE TIP: Layering the sandwich with the avocados and lettuce on the outside, touching the bread, prevents the bread from getting soggy from juices.

Per Serving Calories: 388; Protein: 21g; Total carbohydrates: 41g; Sugars: 8g; Fiber: 6g; Total fat: 16g; Saturated fat: 2g; Cholesterol: 49mg; Sodium: 564mg

Ground Turkey-Stuffed Peppers

EGG-FREE, TREE NUT-FREE, PEANUT-FREE, SOY-FREE

Stuffed peppers are our favorite traditional Italian-style entrée. The simple ingredients, most of which you have on hand, blend together for a hearty, flavorful meal. This is an excellent dish to make in advance and bake just before serving. Simply prep in the morning (skipping the step 2 oven preheat) and refrigerate until dinnertime, then preheat the oven and bake as directed in step 4. If you have leftover rice, it comes together in no time.

- **Prep time: 20 minutes**
- **Cook time: 40 minutes**
- **Serves 4**

½ cup long-grain white rice

4 large green bell peppers

2 to 3 tablespoons olive oil, divided

1 pound ground turkey

8 ounces mushrooms, chopped

4 garlic cloves, minced

1 onion, diced

1 (25-ounce) jar pasta sauce

1½ cups shredded nondairy mozzarella or cheddar cheese, divided

Chopped or torn fresh basil leaves, for garnish (optional)

Salt (preferably pink Himalayan)

Freshly ground black pepper

1. In a small saucepan, cook the rice according to package directions.

2. Preheat the oven to 350°F. Coat a 9-inch baking pan with nonstick cooking spray.

3. Meanwhile, slice off and discard the tops off the peppers. Remove and discard the seeds and membranes. Place the peppers in the prepared pan.

4. In a large skillet, heat 2 tablespoons of oil over medium-high heat. Add the turkey, mushrooms, garlic, and onion. Cook for 10 minutes, or until the turkey is no longer pink, stirring with a wooden spoon to break up the meat. If the turkey begins to stick, add the remaining 1 tablespoon of oil.

5. Add the pasta sauce, 1 cup of cheese, and the cooked rice and stir until just combined. Remove from the heat. Evenly divide the turkey mixture among the peppers. Place any extra mixture around the filled peppers. Sprinkle with the remaining ½ cup of cheese.

6. Bake for 40 to 45 minutes, or until the peppers are tender. Garnish with fresh basil (if using). If desired, season with salt and black pepper to taste.

VARIATION TIP: You can use ground beef or pork in place of turkey and substitute colorful red, orange, or yellow peppers for a sweeter taste than classic green peppers.

Per Serving Calories: 523; Protein: 36g; Total carbohydrates: 47g; Sugars: 13g; Fiber: 8g; Total fat: 22g; Saturated fat: 3g; Cholesterol: 62mg; Sodium: 571mg

Waldorf Chicken Salad Sandwich

EGG-FREE, PEANUT-FREE, SOY-FREE

Here's a healthy chicken salad with pecans and celery for loads of crunch, and juicy grapes for a burst of sweetness. You can easily change it up by using apples, strawberries, or mango in place of the grapes, and walnuts, almonds, or cashews for the pecans. Toasting the nuts, if time permits, adds depth of flavor. If you prefer to skip the bread, use the butter lettuce as a wrap.

- **Prep time: 15 minutes**
- **Serves 4**

½ cup vegan mayonnaise

2 tablespoons freshly squeezed lemon juice

1 tablespoon Dijon mustard

1 scallion, white and green parts, sliced

1 tablespoon chopped fresh thyme

1 tablespoon chopped fresh parsley

Salt (preferably pink Himalayan)

Freshly ground black pepper

2 cups shredded cooked chicken

1 cup red grapes, halved

½ cup pecans, chopped

2 celery stalks, finely diced (about ½ cup)

8 slices gluten-free bread

1 avocado, sliced

8 to 12 large butter lettuce leaves

1. In a large bowl, whisk together the mayonnaise, lemon juice, mustard, scallion, thyme, and parsley, If desired, add salt and pepper to taste. Fold in the chicken, grapes, pecans, and celery.

2. Place 1 slice bread on each of four plates. Evenly divide the chicken salad among the bread slices and top each with one-quarter of the avocado and lettuce. Top with the remaining slices of bread.

Per Serving (1 sandwich) Calories: 581; Protein: 27g; Total carbohydrates: 44g; Sugars: 4g; Fiber: 7g; Total fat: 35g; Saturated fat: 8g; Cholesterol: 54mg; Sodium: 688mg

Apricot-Basil Glazed Turkey Cutlets

EGG-FREE, TREE NUT-FREE, PEANUT-FREE, SOY-FREE

This delicious and simple glaze—made with apricot preserves and fresh basil—perfectly complements tender, mild turkey cutlets. This glaze is not only what makes *this* dish excellent but is also scrumptious on its own, served with leftover turkey or chicken meat any time of the year. Or serve over grilled pork tenderloin or roasted, thick fish fillets, such as grouper, sea bass, or sole.

- **Prep time: 25 minutes**
- **Cook time: 40 minutes**
- **Serves 4**

FOR THE GLAZE

2 tablespoons nondairy butter

4 large fresh basil leaves, plus 2 tablespoons chopped basil, divided

1 (10-ounce) jar apricot preserves

1 tablespoon white balsamic vinegar

¼ teaspoon salt (preferably pink Himalayan)

⅛ teaspoon freshly ground black pepper

FOR THE TURKEY

2 tablespoons nondairy butter

1 pound thinly sliced turkey cutlets

Salt (preferably pink Himalayan)

Freshly ground black pepper

TO MAKE THE GLAZE

1. In a small saucepan, heat the butter over medium heat. Add the basil leaves and cook for 2 to 3 minutes, until the basil becomes fragrant. Discard the basil.

2. Add the preserves, vinegar, salt, and pepper and cook, stirring often, for 1 minute to warm and blend. Stir in the remaining 2 tablespoons of chopped basil. Cover and set aside or refrigerate until ready to use. This can be served warm or cold.

TO MAKE THE TURKEY

1. In a large skillet, heat the butter over medium-high heat. Working in batches, if necessary, to avoid crowding the pan, add the turkey and cook for 2 to 3 minutes total, flipping once, or until cooked through. If desired, season with salt and pepper to taste.

2. Serve the cutlets topped with the glaze.

SUBSTITUTION TIP: If you have trouble finding turkey cutlets, you can make your own or use chicken cutlets instead. Cut boneless, skinless turkey or chicken breasts horizontally into slices ¼ to ½ inch thick.

Per Serving Calories: 417; Protein: 28g; Total carbohydrates: 46g; Sugars: 42g; Fiber: 0g; Total fat: 14g; Saturated fat: 3g; Cholesterol: 45mg; Sodium: 248mg

Rosemary-Sage Infused Turkey Roast with Gravy

EGG-FREE, TREE NUT-FREE, PEANUT-FREE, SOY-FREE

The golden-brown exterior of this turkey comes from roasting the meat at a high temperature to seal in the juices and crisp the skin, then reducing the temperature to finish cooking and absorb the flavors of the herbs stuffed under the skin. We make it this way every holiday season, and it never disappoints. For a nice presentation when serving on a platter, arrange fresh herb sprigs around the roast.

- **Prep time: 35 minutes**
- **Cook time: 3 to 4 hours**
- **Serves 14**

FOR THE TURKEY

1 fresh turkey (14 to 16 pounds)

4 tablespoons nondairy butter, at room temperature

5 rosemary sprigs

5 sage sprigs

5 thyme sprigs

½ teaspoon salt (preferably pink Himalayan)

½ teaspoon freshly ground black pepper

4 cups turkey or chicken broth

FOR THE GRAVY

1 to 2 cups turkey or chicken broth, if needed

3 tablespoons nondairy butter

1 cup onion, diced

¼ cup all-purpose gluten-free flour

½ cup nondairy milk

¾ teaspoon salt (preferably pink Himalayan)

½ teaspoon freshly ground black pepper

¼ cup sherry

TO MAKE THE TURKEY

1. Remove the giblets and neck from the turkey cavity. Place the turkey on a rack in a roasting pan. Evenly rub the butter under the skin and insert the herb sprigs. Sprinkle the skin with the salt and pepper. Add the broth to the bottom of the pan. Let stand at room temperature for 30 minutes.

2. Position a rack in the bottom third of the oven and preheat the oven to 400°F.

3. Transfer the turkey to the oven and roast for 10 to 12 minutes per pound. After 1 hour, reduce the oven temperature to 350°F, cover the turkey with aluminum foil, and continue roasting for 2 hours to 2 hours 45 minutes, or until a thermometer inserted in the center of the breast reaches 170°F and the thighs reach 180°F.

4. Transfer the turkey to a cutting board or serving platter and let rest, tented with foil, for 20 minutes.

TO MAKE THE GRAVY

1. Pour the drippings out of the roasting pan into a fat separator (or measuring cup) and let stand for 5 minutes for the fat to rise to the top. Skim the fat from the top and reserve the broth. Add additional broth if needed to equal 2 cups.

2. In a medium skillet, heat the butter over medium-high heat. Add the onion and cook, stirring, for about 3 minutes, or until slightly translucent.

3. Add the flour and whisk to combine for about 1 minute. Add the broth and milk and whisk to smooth any lumps from the flour. Whisk in the salt, pepper, and sherry. Cook, whisking constantly, for 3 to 5 minutes, or until thickened slightly.

RECIPE TIP: Cut the butter into tablespoons to rub evenly under the entire skin of the bird. If the skin is sticking tightly to the flesh, pull it up a bit. Then stuff the herb sprigs everywhere. This allows for maximum flavor and holds in the flavors to seep through the skin. The result is a mouthwatering and juicy roast!

Per Serving Calories: 255; Protein: 38g; Total carbohydrates: 3g; Sugars: 1g; Fiber: 1g; Total fat: 9g; Saturated fat: 2g; Cholesterol: 118mg; Sodium: 541mg

Pork Chops in Cherry–Wine Sauce

EGG-FREE, TREE NUT-FREE, PEANUT-FREE, SOY-FREE

What's great about pork is that it's leaner than other red meats, and the cherry white wine sauce keeps this dish juicy, tangy, and flavorful. It's delightful served with a side of rice or quinoa and a dab of stone-ground mustard for dipping. Add a premade green salad and you've got dinner in just 20 minutes!

- **Prep time: 5 minutes**
- **Cook time: 15 minutes**
- **Serves 4**

FOR THE PORK CHOPS

1 teaspoon dried basil

1 teaspoon dried thyme

1 teaspoon dried rosemary

4 (1-inch-thick) boneless pork loin chops, trimmed

Salt (preferably pink Himalayan)

Freshly ground black pepper

1 tablespoon extra-virgin olive oil

FOR THE SAUCE

4 tablespoons nondairy butter

1 shallot, minced

1 cup frozen dark sweet cherries, thawed

⅓ cup dry white wine

2 tablespoons sugar

¾ teaspoon salt (preferably pink Himalayan)

½ teaspoon freshly ground black pepper

TO MAKE THE PORK CHOPS

1. In a small bowl, stir together the basil, thyme, and rosemary. Sprinkle the pork chops with salt and pepper to taste and pat the herbs on both sides of the meat.

2. In a large skillet, heat the oil over medium-high heat. Add the pork chops and cook for 6 minutes, turning once, or until browned and a thermometer inserted into the center of a chop reaches 145°F. Transfer the chops to a plate, cover, and keep warm.

TO MAKE THE SAUCE

In the same skillet, melt the butter over medium-high heat. Add the shallot and cook for 1 minute. Add the cherries, wine, sugar, salt, and pepper. Bring to a boil and boil for 1 minute. Reduce the heat to medium and simmer for 3 minutes to reduce the liquid. Serve the pork chops with the sauce.

RECIPE TIP: Pork is delicate and best when cooked just to the required temperature, as overcooking makes it dry and tough. It's also best when it stands for 3 to 5 minutes after cooking, just enough time to make the sauce.

Per Serving Calories: 334; Protein: 21g; Total carbohydrates: 13g; Sugars: 11g; Fiber: 1g; Total fat: 21g; Saturated fat: 3g; Cholesterol: 0mg; Sodium: 440mg

BLT Avocado Sandwich with Cajun Aioli

EGG-FREE, TREE NUT-FREE, PEANUT-FREE, SOY-FREE

Nothing is better than a quick and easy lunch packed with Cajun flavors! Toasting the bread first makes this sandwich extra crispy and delicious, plus it seals in the flavors and prevents the bread from getting soggy. This makes a great dinner especially with a mug of hot soup in cooler months, though I leave out the Cajun sauce when I make it for my kiddos.

- **Prep time: 5 minutes**
- **Cook time: 20 minutes**
- **Serves 4**

10 ounces reduced-sodium turkey bacon

⅓ cup vegan mayonnaise

2 teaspoons yellow mustard

1 teaspoon freshly squeezed lime juice

½ teaspoon Cajun seasoning

8 slices gluten-free bread, toasted

8 to 12 lettuce leaves

1 large beefsteak tomato, sliced

2 avocados, sliced

1. Preheat the oven to 400°F.

2. Place a rack on a rimmed baking sheet and arrange the bacon slices on the rack without touching. Bake for 12 to 18 minutes, or until crisp. Remove from the oven and pat with a paper towel to absorb excess oil.

3. Meanwhile, in a small bowl, whisk together the mayonnaise, mustard, lime juice, and Cajun seasoning. Set aside.

4. Place 1 slice of toast on each of 4 plates. Evenly divide the mayonnaise mixture, lettuce, tomato slices, bacon, and avocado among the toasts. Top with the remaining slices of toast.

INGREDIENT TIP: The bacon can be cooked in a skillet or in the microwave. If cooking in the microwave, check two-thirds of the way through the cook time for desired level of doneness.

Per Serving Calories: 528; Protein: 12g; Total carbohydrates: 44g; Sugars: 7g; Fiber: 8g; Total fat: 37g; Saturated fat: 4g; Cholesterol: 25mg; Sodium: 740mg

Glazed Apple Pork Kebabs with Pear Chutney

EGG-FREE, TREE NUT-FREE, PEANUT-FREE, SOY-FREE

Pork pairs well with seasonal fruits, as highlighted in this recipe featuring apple butter in the marinade and a sweet pear chutney as an accompaniment. This chutney is also great for any appetizer or charcuterie board, spread over crackers with Vegan Ricotta Cheese (page 166). You can easily change up the fruit in this recipe to use whatever is in peak season; try peaches, plums, or persimmons. It's also delicious served with Autumn Greens Salad (page 34).

- **Prep time: 25 minutes, plus 1 hour to marinate**
- **Cook time: 12 minutes**
- **Serves 4**

FOR THE PORK

1½ pounds boneless pork loin, trimmed and cut into 1-inch cubes

1 cup store-bought apple butter

FOR THE CHUTNEY

5 pears, peeled, cored, and chopped

⅔ cup finely chopped red bell pepper

¾ cup coconut sugar

½ cup finely diced onion

¼ cup dried currants

1 (1-inch) piece fresh ginger, minced

¼ cup white wine vinegar

¼ cup orange juice

½ tablespoon freshly squeezed lemon juice

½ teaspoon ground nutmeg

½ teaspoon ground cinnamon

¼ teaspoon salt (preferably pink Himalayan)

FOR THE KEBABS

½ red onion, diced

1 red bell pepper, diced

TO PREPARE THE PORK

1. Soak 4 wooden skewers in water for 1 hour prior to grilling.
2. Place the pork in a large bowl and toss with the apple butter. Cover and refrigerate for at least 1 hour or up to 4 hours to marinate.

TO MAKE THE CHUTNEY

In a large saucepan, combine pears, bell pepper, sugar, onion, currants, ginger, and vinegar. Bring to a boil over high heat. Reduce the heat to low and simmer, uncovered, for 20 minutes, stirring occasionally, until thickened. Stir in the orange juice, lemon juice, nutmeg, cinnamon, and salt. Over medium heat, return the mixture to a simmer and cook, stirring occasionally, for 5 minutes to allow the flavors to blend. Set aside until ready to use.

1. Coat the grill grates with nonstick cooking spray. Preheat the grill to medium.

2. Thread the pork onto the soaked skewers with the red onion and red bell peppers, dividing evenly and leaving ¼ inch space between the pieces.

3. Place the skewers on the grill and cook for 10 to 12 minutes, turning once, or until the meat is just slightly pink in the center.

4. Serve the kebabs with the chutney.

VARIATION TIP: Instead of grilling, you can pan-sear the pork in 1 tablespoon olive oil over medium-high heat for 8 to 10 minutes, turning often, until cooked through. To shave off some prep time, instead of the pork roast, look for 1-inch-thick boneless pork loin chops and cut them into 1-inch cubes.

Per Serving Calories: 665; Protein: 34g; Total carbohydrates: 109g; Sugars: 90g; Fiber: 9g; Total fat: 13g; Saturated fat: 5g; Cholesterol: 82mg; Sodium: 760mg

Roasted Beef Tenderloin with Roasted Potatoes, Figs, Carrots, and Fennel

EGG-FREE, TREE NUT-FREE, PEANUT-FREE, SOY-FREE

This juicy roast is bursting with robust flavors and a side of autumn figs, fennel, and hearty potatoes. For a springtime roast, use small golden potatoes, red onion wedges, thick asparagus, and honey, reducing the roasting time to 15 minutes. Either way, roasting the vegetables makes an easy side dish without extra cleanup while bringing out the natural sweetness and flavors of fresh produce. This one is sure to be a meat-lover's favorite meal!

- **Prep time: 15 minutes, plus 10 minutes to stand**
- **Cook time: 50 minutes**
- **Serves 4**

2 teaspoons salt (preferably pink Himalayan)

2 teaspoons freshly ground black pepper

1 teaspoon garlic powder

1 teaspoon onion powder

1 tablespoon herbes de Provence

6 tablespoons avocado oil or extra-virgin olive oil, divided

2 pounds center-cut beef tenderloin, trimmed

4 Yukon Gold potatoes, cut into 1-inch cubes

8 fresh figs, halved

2 cups baby carrots

1 fennel bulb, trimmed and sliced

1 tablespoon maple syrup

½ teaspoon salt (preferably pink Himalayan)

½ teaspoon freshly ground black pepper

2 tablespoons chopped fresh chives, for garnish

1. Preheat the oven to 400°F. Coat a large rimmed baking sheet with nonstick cooking spray.

2. In a small bowl, stir together the salt, pepper, garlic powder, onion powder, herbes de Provence, and 1 tablespoon of oil. Rub the seasoning over the meat to fully coat.

3. In a large ovenproof skillet, preferably cast iron, heat 3 tablespoons of oil over high heat until hot. Add the beef and cook for 5 minutes, to sear all sides.

4. Transfer to the oven and roast for 35 to 45 minutes, turning once, or until the internal temperature reaches 135°F for medium-rare. Remove from the oven and cover lightly with aluminum foil. Let rest for 10 minutes before slicing.

5. Meanwhile, in a large bowl, toss together the potatoes, figs, carrots, and fennel. Add the remaining 2 tablespoons of oil, the maple syrup, salt, and pepper. Arrange the potato mixture on the baking sheet. Roast for 30 minutes, flip, and roast an additional 15 to 20 minutes, or until browned and tender. Remove from the oven and keep warm.

6. Place the beef and vegetables on a serving platter and garnish with the chives.

SUBSTITUTION TIP: If you have trouble finding fresh figs or do not want fruit, use ½ pound halved Brussels sprouts. Or leave them out altogether.

Per Serving Calories: 748; Protein: 57g; Total carbohydrates: 53g; Sugars: 19g; Fiber: 8g; Total fat: 36g; Saturated fat: 9g; Cholesterol: 152mg; Sodium: 1,643mg

One-Pan Beef and Pepper Potato Hash

EGG-FREE, TREE NUT-FREE, PEANUT-FREE, SOY-FREE

I made this beef for dinner one night while my mom was visiting, and my family raved about how perfectly cooked the meat was! Searing the meat before roasting locks in the juices. I highly suggest getting a cast iron skillet for searing meats, which helps provide a crisp crust and tender center. Roasting the beef for only 8 minutes will result in a medium-rare center; cook it longer for more well done.

- **Prep time: 15 minutes**
- **Cook time: 20 minutes**
- **Serves 4**

2 (6-ounce) top sirloin steaks, trimmed

Salt (preferably pink Himalayan)

Freshly ground black pepper

2 tablespoons nondairy butter

1 tablespoon extra-virgin olive oil

1 red bell pepper, cut into thin strips, then halve the strips

1 green bell pepper, thinly sliced, then halved

2 small Yukon Gold potatoes, shredded

1 sweet onion, chopped

Fresh parsley or cilantro, for garnish

1. Preheat the oven to 400°F.

2. If desired, season the steaks with salt and pepper to taste.

3. In a cast iron or other oven-proof skillet, heat the butter over medium-high heat. Add the steaks and cook for 3 minutes, or until browned. Flip and cook 1 minute longer to brown. Transfer the skillet to the oven and roast for 8 minutes, or until a thermometer inserted in the center of the steaks reaches 135°F for medium-rare. Transfer the meat to a plate and let rest 10 minutes before cutting into small pieces.

4. In the same skillet, heat the oil over medium heat. Add the bell peppers, potatoes, and onion. Cook, covered, for 8 minutes, stirring once, until the vegetables are tender. Stir in the steak during the last minute of cooking. Garnish with the parsley.

VARIATION TIP: To change it up, use boneless, skinless chicken thighs or boneless pork chops for the beef. Have any leftovers? This is also a wonderful dish to turn into tacos or serve on top of chips baked with nondairy cheese.

Per Serving Calories: 303; Protein: 22g; Total carbohydrates: 23g; Sugars: 5g; Fiber: 4g; Total fat: 14g; Saturated fat: 2g; Cholesterol: 63mg; Sodium: 129mg

Loaded Beef Quesadillas
with Avocado Salsa

EGG-FREE, TREE NUT-FREE, PEANUT-FREE, SOY-FREE

Family quesadilla nights just got an upgrade with this delicious avocado salsa that's packed with protein and veggies. Serve the crispy, cheesy bites as a meal or mini appetizer.

- **Prep time: 15 minutes**
- **Cook time: 20 minutes**
- **Serves 4**

FOR THE SALSA

3 firm-ripe avocados, diced

1 cup frozen corn kernels, thawed

1 cup canned black beans, drained and rinsed

¼ cup finely diced red bell pepper

¼ cup finely diced red onion

½ cup salsa

2 tablespoons chopped fresh cilantro

Salt (preferably pink Himalayan)

Freshly ground black pepper

FOR THE QUESADILLAS

8 gluten-free tortillas or 16 corn tortillas

1 cup shredded nondairy Cheddar cheese

1 cup finely diced cooked beef sirloin or roast

4 teaspoons mild gluten-free taco seasoning (low sodium, if desired)

Preheat the oven to 170°F. Coat a baking sheet with nonstick cooking spray and place in the oven.

TO MAKE THE SALSA

In a medium bowl, stir together the avocados, corn, beans, bell pepper, onion, salsa, and cilantro. If desired, season with salt and black pepper to taste. Set aside.

TO MAKE THE QUESADILLAS

1. Coat a skillet with nonstick cooking spray, then heat over medium-high heat. Place 1 tortilla in the skillet. Sprinkle with ¼ cup of cheese, ¼ cup of beef, and a bit of the taco seasoning. Top with a second tortilla. Heat for 4 to 5 minutes, flipping once, or until browned and the cheese melts. Place on the baking sheet to keep warm. Repeat to make 3 more quesadillas.

2. To serve, cut each quesadilla into 4 wedges. Top with the salsa.

VARIATION TIP: This meal can be tweaked by using cooked pork roast, grilled chicken, or steamed shrimp. Use leftovers or cook the meat or seafood just before making the quesadillas.

Per Serving Calories: 783; Protein: 31g; Total carbohydrates: 88g; Sugars: 9g; Fiber: 17g; Total fat: 40g; Saturated fat: 12g; Cholesterol: 50mg; Sodium: 1,415mg

Sweet and Sour Beef and Peppers

EGG-FREE, PEANUT-FREE, SOY-FREE

Here's a healthy, easy Chinese-inspired beef dish that you can have ready faster than takeout without the worry about cross-contamination. Made without breading, the beef is delicious coated with a thick sauce bursting with sweet notes and umami flavors. Not only is the sauce good on beef, it makes an excellent topping for sautéed or steamed vegetables. Serve this over hot cooked rice for a complete meal.

- **Prep time: 10 minutes**
- **Cook time: 15 minutes**
- **Serves 4**

FOR THE SAUCE

1 tablespoon cornstarch

1 tablespoon water

¾ cup coconut sugar

½ cup apple cider vinegar

⅓ cup ketchup

¼ cup coconut aminos or gluten-free soy sauce

1½ tablespoons toasted sesame oil

1 beef bouillon cube

3 garlic cloves, minced

FOR THE BEEF

¼ cup cornstarch

½ teaspoon paprika

Salt (preferably pink Himalayan)

Freshly ground black pepper

1¼ pounds beef stew meat, cut into 1-inch pieces

2 tablespoons extra-virgin olive oil

1 red bell pepper, cut into 1-inch pieces

1 green bell pepper, cut into 1-inch pieces

½ cup snow peas

1 scallion, green parts only, sliced (optional)

Sesame seeds (optional)

TO MAKE THE SAUCE

1. In a small bowl, whisk together the cornstarch and water.

2. In a medium saucepan, stir together the coconut sugar, vinegar, ketchup, coconut aminos, sesame oil, bouillon, and garlic. Bring to a simmer over medium heat, then reduce the heat to low. Stir in the cornstarch mixture and simmer for 3 minutes, or until thickened. Cover and set the sauce aside.

TO MAKE THE BEEF

1. In a zip-top bag, combine the cornstarch, paprika, and a dash of salt and black pepper and shake to blend well. Add the beef, seal the bag, and shake until the beef is coated.

2. In a large nonstick skillet, heat the oil over medium-high heat. Add the beef and cook, stirring, for 5 minutes. Move to the side of the skillet and add the bell peppers, snow peas, and any cornstarch mixture left in the bag and cook, stirring, for 4 minutes, or until the vegetables are tender-crisp.

3. Stir the sweet and sour sauce into the skillet and cook, stirring, for 2 minutes, or until thickened and heated through. Top with the scallion and sesame seeds (if using).

VARIATION TIP: For a vegetarian version, instead of the beef, drain a 16-ounce package of extra-firm tofu. Line a sieve with paper towel, add the tofu, and set a plate on top. Place a heavy can on the plate and let stand for 30 minutes to release the liquid. Discard the liquid and cut the tofu into 1-inch cubes. Sauté the tofu in the oil. Remove from the pan, cook the vegetables, then return to the pan when you add the sweet and sour sauce.

Per Serving Calories: 595; Protein: 39g; Total carbohydrates: 61g; Sugars: 44g; Fiber: 2g; Total fat: 23g; Saturated fat: 2g; Cholesterol: 51mg; Sodium: 413mg

Roast Beef with Garlic Herb Spread

EGG-FREE, PEANUT-FREE, SOY-FREE

The trick to a great roast beef is to start the meat at high temperature to sear it, and then finish at a lower temperature. Cooking on low heat allows the flavors to marry, resulting in a juicier and more tender meat. Serve this roast with mashed, roasted, or steamed potatoes with a side of steamed vegetables such as asparagus, broccoli, or green beans. The vegetables will sing when topped with a dollop of the garlic herb spread.

- **Prep time: 20 minutes, plus 1 hour to marinate**
- **Cook time: 2 hours**
- **Serves 10**

FOR THE MARINADE

½ cup extra-virgin olive oil

½ cup coconut aminos or gluten-free soy sauce

¼ cup apple cider vinegar

4 garlic cloves, minced

2 tablespoons chopped fresh thyme

1 tablespoon chopped fresh rosemary

2 bay leaves

½ teaspoon salt (preferably pink Himalayan)

½ teaspoon freshly ground black pepper

3 pounds beef eye round roast, trimmed

FOR THE SPREAD

1 cup (2 sticks) nondairy butter, at room temperature

Juice of 1 lemon

1 garlic clove, minced

1 tablespoon chopped fresh parsley

1 tablespoon chopped fresh basil

1 tablespoon chopped fresh rosemary

1 teaspoon salt (preferably pink Himalayan)

TO MAKE THE MARINADE

1. In a small bowl, stir together the oil, coconut aminos, vinegar, garlic, thyme, rosemary, bay leaves, salt, and pepper.

2. Place the roast in a large roasting pan. Pour the marinade over the meat, cover, and refrigerate for at least 1 hour or up to overnight, flipping occasionally.

TO MAKE THE SPREAD

1. Preheat the oven to 400°F.

2. In a medium bowl, with an electric mixer, beat the butter, lemon juice, garlic, parsley, basil, rosemary, and salt until well blended. Cover and refrigerate until ready to use.

TO ROAST AND SERVE THE BEEF

1. Transfer the roasting pan to the oven and roast the beef in the marinade for 20 minutes. Reduce the oven temperature to 325°F. Roast for 1 hour 30 minutes longer, or until a thermometer inserted in the center of the roast reaches 135°F for medium-rare. Remove from the oven and let stand, tented in foil, for 15 to 30 minutes.

2. Slice and serve topped with a dab of the garlic herb spread.

RECIPE TIP: This roast makes enough for leftovers in most families. We love to use leftover roast beef in sandwiches. Spread some of the garlic herb spread on gluten-free rolls and top with thin slices of the beef.

Per Serving Calories: 636; Protein: 27g; Total carbohydrates: 4g; Sugars: <1g; Fiber: <1g; Total fat: 56g; Saturated fat: 16g; Cholesterol: 48mg; Sodium: 1,269mg

Top Sirloin Steak with Roasted Rosemary Potatoes and Carrots

EGG-FREE, TREE NUT-FREE, PEANUT-FREE, SOY-FREE

There's nothing better than tender steak with a buttery crisp exterior and rich, juicy flavors. This hearty steak is served with flavorful, herb-infused roasted potatoes and carrots; but any blend of seasonal veggies will be delicious—try turnips, sweet potatoes, or butternut squash in the cooler months, or a blend of zucchini, eggplant, and red bell pepper in the warmer months.

- **Prep time: 20 minutes, plus 10 minutes to rest**
- **Cook time: 45 minutes**
- **Serves 4**

4 (6-ounce) top sirloin steaks, trimmed

Pinch of salt (preferably pink Himalayan), plus 1 teaspoon, divided

Pinch freshly ground black pepper, plus ½ teaspoon, divided

4 Yukon Gold potatoes, cut into 1-inch pieces

4 large carrots, cut into 1-inch pieces

2 tablespoons extra-virgin olive oil

¼ cup chopped fresh rosemary

2 tablespoons chopped fresh oregano

4 tablespoons nondairy butter, melted

2 garlic cloves, minced

1. Place the steaks on a plate and sprinkle with a pinch of salt and pepper. Set aside to come to room temperature.

2. Preheat the oven to 400°F.

3. In a large bowl, combine the potatoes, carrots, oil, rosemary, oregano, 1 teaspoon salt, and the remaining ½ teaspoon of pepper. Toss to coat well. Spread in a single layer on a large rimmed baking sheet. Bake for 40 to 45 minutes, stirring once, until the vegetables are nice and crispy on the outside.

4. Meanwhile, in a small bowl, whisk together the melted butter and garlic. With a basting brush, coat the steaks with some of the garlic butter. Pour any remaining butter into a large cast iron skillet and heat over medium-high heat. Add the steaks and cook for 3 minutes, or until browned on the first side. Flip and cook 1 minute longer to brown on the second side. Transfer the skillet to the oven and roast for 8 minutes, or until a thermometer inserted in the center of the steaks reaches 135°F for medium-rare. Let rest on the counter for 5 to 10 minutes or until the vegetables are done.

5. Place the steak and vegetables on a platter and serve.

RECIPE TIP: Don't overcook this leaner cut of steak or it will be tough and chewy. Letting the meat rest ensures a juicy, tender steak because it allows the juices to distribute into the meat and not run out too quickly when you cut into it.

Per Serving Calories: 607; Protein: 44g; Total carbohydrates: 45g; Sugars: 6g; Fiber: 9g; Total fat: 28g; Saturated fat: 4g; Cholesterol: 45mg; Sodium: 937mg

Zuppa Toscana

EGG-FREE, PEANUT-FREE, SOY-FREE

Zuppa toscana literally means "Tuscan soup." It's traditionally made with kale, zucchini, cannellini beans, potatoes, celery, carrots, onion, and tomatoes and served with toasted Tuscan bread. This version is bursting with meat flavor from bacon and Italian sausage but still features plenty of kale and potatoes. If desired, serve with gluten-free ciabatta or French rolls.

- **Prep time: 15 minutes**
- **Cook time: 35 minutes**
- **Serves 6**

6 bacon slices, cut into bite-size pieces

1 pound spicy Italian sausage meat

1 onion, diced

3 garlic cloves, minced

5 cups chicken broth

5 medium Yukon Gold potatoes, diced

½ teaspoon chili powder

Salt (preferably pink Himalayan)

Freshly ground black pepper

4 cups chopped kale

1 cup canned full-fat coconut milk

½ cup nutritional yeast, plus more (optional) for serving

1. In a large saucepan, cook the bacon over medium-high heat for 10 minutes, stirring often, until browned. Place a paper towel on a plate and top with the cooked bacon. Place another paper towel on top and pat to absorb any extra oil. Break up the bacon into crumbles. Discard the bacon drippings.

2. In the same saucepan, cook the sausage over medium-high heat for 5 minutes, stirring with a wooden spoon to break up the meat, until browned. Add the onion and cook, stirring, for 5 minutes, or until translucent. Stir in the garlic and cook for 1 minute.

3. Add the broth, potatoes, chili powder, and a dash each of salt and pepper. Bring to a simmer, reduce the heat to medium-low, cover, and simmer for 10 minutes, or until the potatoes are tender. Stir in the kale, bacon, coconut milk, and nutritional yeast and simmer for 5 minutes to blend the flavors.

4. Serve with extra nutritional yeast on top, if desired.

SIMPLIFY IT: This recipe can be made in advance and eaten the next day, which makes it even more flavorful. You can also use turkey bacon and turkey sausage to reduce the amount of fat and cholesterol.

Per Serving Calories: 486; Protein: 22g; Total carbohydrates: 47g; Sugars: 3g; Fiber: 10g; Total fat: 21g; Saturated fat: 11g; Cholesterol: 33mg; Sodium: 951mg

Snacks

Herb-Infused Beet Hummus, page **135**

No-Bake Peanut Butter Chia Energy Bars

EGG-FREE, TREE NUT-FREE, SOY-FREE, VEGAN

I shared this recipe with friends years ago and, to my surprise, one day when I showed up at the park with my kids, a friend pulled out a bag filled with these snacks and told me she makes my recipe often, as it is her go-to healthy snack. Guess what, it is ours, too, and I hope it becomes yours as well! If you have a peanut allergy, you can use almond, cashew, or sunflower seed butter.

- **Prep time: 10 minutes, plus 15 to 30 minutes to set**
- **Makes 12 bars**

½ cup peanut butter

⅓ cup maple syrup or honey

1½ cups gluten-free quick-cooking oats

½ cup all-purpose gluten-free flour

1 tablespoon chia seeds

1 to 2 tablespoons apple juice

1 tablespoon vanilla extract

1 teaspoon ground cinnamon

Salt (preferably pink Himalayan)

½ cup dairy-free semisweet chocolate chips

1. In a large microwave-safe bowl, combine the peanut butter and maple syrup. Microwave on high for 30 seconds, or until softened. Whisk together until smooth.

2. Add the oats, flour, chia seeds, 1 tablespoon of apple juice, the vanilla, cinnamon, and a dash of salt. Stir to coat well. Add the chocolate chips and stir to combine. Knead the mixture, adding another 1 tablespoon of apple juice if needed, until well blended and the oats absorb the liquid.

3. Line a baking sheet with parchment paper and top with the mixture. Add a sheet of parchment paper on top and roll the dough into a square about ½ inch thick. Place in refrigerator for about 30 minutes or in the freezer for 15 minutes, or until firm.

4. Remove from the refrigerator and slice into about 6 strips, then cut each strip in half. Store in the refrigerator in an airtight container lined with parchment paper for up to 3 days.

INGREDIENT TIP: If the peanut butter is unsalted, add a pinch more salt to the recipe (taste as you stir the mixture).

VARIATION TIP: If desired, instead of bars, roll the mixture into 1-inch balls. Store in an airtight container in the refrigerator.

Per Serving (1 bar) Calories: 216; Protein: 6g; Total carbohydrates: 29g; Sugars: 9g; Fiber: 2g; Total fat: 10g; Saturated fat: 3g; Cholesterol: 0mg; Sodium: 64mg

Chocolate-Covered Cherry Trail Mix

EGG-FREE, PEANUT-FREE, SOY-FREE, VEGETARIAN

Perfect for hiking, afterschool snacks, a late-night nosh for the family, or even to wrap in individual baggies for bake sales, this mix is ready in a moment's time. If you have a hard time finding cherries, any dried fruit will work. Try mixing it up with golden raisins and diced apricots. This is also delicious over yogurt, ice cream, or Peanut Butter and Chocolate Swirl Overnight Oats (page 28), for extra crunch.

- **Prep time: 5 minutes**
- **Cook time: 15 minutes**
- **Serves 4**

1 cup salted roasted almonds

1 cup salted roasted cashews

1 cup salted roasted sunflower seeds

½ cup pecans

½ cup dried cherries

¼ cup honey

2 tablespoons coconut oil, melted

⅓ cup dairy-free chocolate chips

1. Preheat the oven to 325°F. Coat a 9-by-13-inch baking dish with nonstick cooking spray.

2. In a large bowl, stir together the almonds, cashews, sunflower seeds, pecans, cherries, honey, and oil. Spread the nut mixture in a single layer in the prepared dish. Bake for 15 minutes to toast slightly, stirring twice to prevent burning.

3. Meanwhile, place the chocolate chips in a microwave-safe bowl and microwave in 30-second increments, stirring well after each, until melted.

4. When the nuts are done, drizzle with the melted chocolate. Place in the refrigerator to harden. Break into chunks.

SIMPLIFY IT: Using salted, roasted nuts keeps this snack simple while bringing out bursts of flavor from the nuts, cherries, honey, and chocolate.

Per Serving Calories: 960; Protein: 24g; Total carbohydrates: 65g; Sugars: 30g; Fiber: 10g; Total fat: 71g; Saturated fat: 17g; Cholesterol: 0mg; Sodium: 543mg

Roasted Curried Chickpeas

EGG-FREE, TREE NUT-FREE, PEANUT-FREE, SOY-FREE, VEGAN

These little snacks satisfy a salty craving. They are simple to roast, lightly flavored with seasonings, and a wholesome snack that adds protein and fiber to your diet. I love putting them in my kids' lunches for a fun, healthy snack. They are also a delicious addition to salads, providing the texture and crunch of croutons but without the grains.

- **Prep time: 10 minutes**
- **Cook time: 40 minutes**
- **Serves 8**

1 (15-ounce can) chickpeas, drained and rinsed

¾ teaspoon ground cumin

¾ teaspoon ground turmeric

¾ teaspoon paprika

½ teaspoon garlic powder

½ teaspoon salt (preferably pink Himalayan)

¼ teaspoon freshly ground black pepper

¼ teaspoon onion powder

¼ teaspoon chili powder

¼ teaspoon ground celery seed

1 tablespoon extra-virgin olive oil

1. Preheat the oven to 375°F. Coat a rimmed baking sheet with nonstick cooking spray.

2. Place the chickpeas on a clean kitchen towel to dry thoroughly. Spread on the prepared baking sheet and bake for 30 minutes, stirring halfway.

3. Meanwhile, in a small bowl, stir together the cumin, turmeric, paprika, garlic powder, salt, pepper, onion powder, chili powder, and celery seed.

4. Remove the baking sheet from the oven and drizzle with the oil and seasoning. Toss to coat well. Return to the oven and bake for 10 to 15 minutes longer, or until crispy.

INGREDIENT TIP: Make sure the chickpeas are nice and dry before they are baked; otherwise, they will not turn out as crunchy. If you have the time, let them air-dry for 30 minutes on the kitchen towel.

Per Serving Calories: 41; Protein: 1g; Total carbohydrates: 5g; Sugars: 1g; Fiber: 0g; Total fat: 2g; Saturated fat: 0g; Cholesterol: 0mg; Sodium: 190mg

Oven-Baked Sweet Potato Fries

EGG-FREE, TREE NUT-FREE, PEANUT-FREE, SOY-FREE, VEGAN

While not the healthiest of foods to eat, I'm a sucker for fries. And I don't enjoy them when eating out, as they're most likely not gluten-free due to cross-contamination. I make these all the time for a healthy snack or easy side dish. These fries are cut into thick wedges, giving them a soft center that is so satisfying. If you are not a sweet potato fan, you can also use russets or Yukon Gold potatoes.

- **Prep time: 10 minutes**
- **Cook time: 20 minutes**
- **Serves 4**

2 large sweet potatoes, scrubbed and dried

3 tablespoons avocado oil

½ teaspoon salt (preferably pink Himalayan)

½ teaspoon freshly ground black pepper

½ teaspoon chili powder (optional)

1. Preheat the oven to 400°F. Coat a baking sheet with nonstick cooking spray.

2. Halve the sweet potatoes lengthwise and cut each half lengthwise into 6 wedges. Place the sweet potatoes in a large bowl and add the oil, salt, pepper, and chili powder (if using). Toss to coat well.

3. Arrange the wedges on the baking sheet. Bake for 20 minutes, turning once, until crisp on both sides.

VARIATION TIP: Sub out the chili powder for ½ teaspoon of gluten-free taco seasoning mix or ½ teaspoon each chopped fresh rosemary and thyme to switch up the flavors.

Per Serving Calories: 149; Protein: 1g; Total carbohydrates: 13g; Sugars: 3g; Fiber: 2g; Total fat: 11g; Saturated fat: 1g; Cholesterol: 0mg; Sodium: 327mg

Herb-Infused Beet Hummus

EGG-FREE, TREE NUT-FREE, PEANUT-FREE, SOY-FREE, VEGAN

This twist on traditional hummus is bursting with fresh herbs, chickpeas, beets, and tahini. Children love dips, and this is a bright, colorful way to provide them a nourishing snack with vegetables for dipping. Serve it at your next dinner party, brunch, or happy hour with friends!

- **Prep time: 10 minutes**
- **Makes 2 cups**

1 (15-ounce) can chickpeas, drained and rinsed

½ cup diced roasted beets (about 2 small)

⅓ cup freshly squeezed lemon juice

2 tablespoons tahini

3 tablespoons olive oil, divided

2 teaspoons chopped fresh basil

2 teaspoons chopped fresh tarragon

2 teaspoons chopped fresh chives

2 teaspoons chopped fresh mint

2 garlic cloves

¾ teaspoon salt, (preferably pink Himalayan)

¼ teaspoon freshly ground black pepper

1. In a food processor or blender, combine the chickpeas, beets, lemon juice, tahini, 2 tablespoons of oil, the basil, tarragon, chives, mint, and garlic. Process until smooth. Season with the salt and pepper.

2. Transfer to a serving bowl and drizzle with the remaining 1 tablespoon of oil.

SUBSTITUTION TIP: Not a fan of beets? Leave them out or use ½ cup fresh spinach, drained roasted red peppers, or canned pumpkin in their place.

Per Serving (¼ cup) Calories: 133; Protein: 4g; Total carbohydrates: 12g; Sugars: 4g; Fiber: 3g; Total fat: 8g; Saturated fat: 1g; Cholesterol: 0mg; Sodium: 245mg

Chickpea Cookie Dough Dip

EGG-FREE, PEANUT-FREE, SOY-FREE, VEGAN

Satisfy a sweet tooth with this delicious and healthy snack packed with fiber and protein from chickpeas. And picky kids will never know it's good for them. It's one of my kids' favorites, both to eat and help make!

- **Prep time: 15 minutes**
- **Serves 6**

1 (15-ounce) can chickpeas, drained and rinsed

½ cup coconut sugar

¼ teaspoon ground cinnamon

⅛ teaspoon salt (preferably pink Himalayan)

¼ cup almond butter

1 tablespoon unsweetened almond milk

2 teaspoons vanilla extract

1 tablespoon coconut oil, melted

½ cup dairy-free mini chocolate chips

1 apple, cored and sliced

2 celery stalks, cut into sticks

½ cup baby carrots

1. In a food processor, combine the chickpeas, coconut sugar, cinnamon, and salt. Blend for 30 seconds. Add the almond butter, milk, vanilla, and oil. Blend until smooth.

2. Scoop into a bowl. Fold in the mini chocolate chips. Serve with sliced apples, celery sticks, and carrots.

INGREDIENT TIP: Make sure to drain and rinse the chickpeas thoroughly to remove the thick liquid in the can. You can reserve the liquid (aquafaba) for use in other recipes.

Per Serving Calories: 195; Protein: 4g; Total carbohydrates: 38g; Sugars: 25g; Fiber: 5g; Total fat: 4g; Saturated fat: 1g; Cholesterol: 0mg; Sodium: 63mg

Chocolate Chip and Spinach Muffins

TREE NUT-FREE, PEANUT-FREE, SOY-FREE, VEGETARIAN

These healthy muffins are green from spinach, which also adds potassium, calcium, iron, and vitamin A to these tender bites. They are bursting with creamy melted chocolate, which disguises the spinach with rich flavor, in this fun way to sneak vegetables into foods where you (and kiddos!) least expect it.

- **Prep time: 10 minutes**
- **Cook time: 20 minutes**
- **Makes 12 muffins**

2 cups packed baby spinach

2 large eggs

¾ cup maple syrup

½ cup unsweetened applesauce

¼ cup avocado oil

2 teaspoons vanilla extract

1½ cups all-purpose gluten-free flour

½ cup tapioca flour

1 teaspoon baking powder

½ teaspoon baking soda

½ teaspoon salt (preferably pink Himalayan)

1 cup dairy-free chocolate chips

1. Preheat the oven to 350°F. Line a muffin pan with paper liners and coat the liners with nonstick cooking spray.

2. In a food processor or blender, combine the spinach, eggs, maple syrup, applesauce, oil, and vanilla. Blend until completely smooth.

3. In a large bowl, stir together the gluten-free flour, tapioca flour, baking powder, baking soda, and salt. Add the spinach mixture and stir just until combined. Fold in the chocolate chips.

4. Evenly divide the mixture among the muffin cups. Bake for 18 to 22 minutes, or until a toothpick inserted in the center of a muffin comes out clean. Let cool for 10 minutes in the pan before transferring to a wire rack to cool. Store in an airtight container and consume within 2 days.

Per Serving (1 muffin) Calories: 211; Protein: 4g; Total carbohydrates: 33g; Sugars: 16g; Fiber: 1g; Total fat: 8g; Saturated fat: 2g; Cholesterol: 31mg; Sodium: 175mg

Pecan-Crusted Vegan Herb Cheese Ball

EGG-FREE, PEANUT-FREE, SOY-FREE, VEGAN

Whether it's a small or large gathering, everyone loves a cheese ball! Simply process the vegan cream cheese with herbs and lemon juice, form into a ball, and coat with pecans. For the holidays or sports, form the ball into a heart shape, Christmas tree, or football to match the theme of the party.

- **Prep time: 10 minutes, plus 4 hours to chill**
- **Serves 12**

3 (8-ounce) containers nondairy cream cheese

1 tablespoon chopped fresh tarragon

1 tablespoon chopped fresh chives

1 tablespoon freshly squeezed lemon juice

1½ cups chopped pecans

1. In a food processor, pulse the cream cheese, tarragon, chives, and lemon juice until smooth. Transfer to an airtight container and refrigerate for 4 hours to firm.

2. Once chilled, shape the mixture into a ball.

3. Place a piece of parchment paper on the counter and arrange the pecans on the paper in a thin layer. Place the ball on the nuts and roll until fully covered. Cover with plastic wrap and place in the refrigerator until ready to serve.

Per Serving Calories: 277; Protein: 6g; Total carbohydrates: 8g; Sugars: 3g; Fiber: 6g; Total fat: 26g; Saturated fat: 7g; Cholesterol: 0mg; Sodium: 230mg

Crunchy Fruit and Nut Granola Bars with Chocolate Drizzle

PEANUT-FREE, SOY-FREE, VEGETARIAN

Sometimes we make this family favorite with dried fruit, and sometimes we leave it out. Forget buying packaged crunchy granola bars—this recipe is the best home-made version, and is healthier, customizable, and less expensive.

- **Prep time: 10 minutes**
- **Cook time: 20 minutes**
- **Makes 12 bars**

1½ cups gluten-free rolled oats

½ cup puffed millet cereal

½ cup unsweetened coconut flakes

1 cup chopped slivered almonds

1 cup chopped pecans

1 cup raw pumpkin seeds

½ cup raisins

½ cup dried cranberries

1 teaspoon vanilla extract

1 teaspoon baking powder

1 teaspoon ground cinnamon

¼ teaspoon ground ginger

¼ teaspoon salt (preferably pink Himalayan)

1 cup honey

6 tablespoons coconut butter

1 cup dairy-free chocolate chips

1. Line a 9-by-9-inch baking dish with parchment paper.

2. In a large bowl, combine the oats, cereal, coconut, almonds, pecans, pumpkin seeds, raisins, cranberries, vanilla, baking powder, cinnamon, ginger, and salt.

3. In a small saucepan over high heat, bring the honey and butter to a boil. Pour over the oat and nut mixture and mix with a spatula until coated. Transfer to the prepared baking dish and press down with your hands to fill the space.

4. Melt the chocolate chips in a microwave for about 30 seconds or until slightly melted. Mix to continue to melt, then drizzle on top of the bars. Cover and set in the refrigerator to chill. Once chilled, cut into bars and store in an airtight container at room temperature or in the refrigerator.

RECIPE TIP: For a softer bar, leave at room temperature. For a slightly harder bar, store in the refrigerator.

Per Serving (1 bar) Calories: 511; Protein: 10g; Total carbohydrates: 58g; Sugars: 41g; Fiber: 7g; Total fat: 30g; Saturated fat: 11g; Cholesterol: 0mg; Sodium: 129mg

Snow White Snacks

EGG-FREE, SOY-FREE, VEGAN

This sweet and crunchy treat is commonly known as "puppy chow." Made with naturally gluten-free Rice Chex cereal coated with dairy-free chocolate and peanut butter, this version adds salted nuts to the mix for a sweet and salty surprise! It's fun to make during the holidays to give as gifts in mason jars.

- **Prep time: 15 minutes**
- **Cook time: 2 minutes**
- **Makes 6 cups**

1 cup confectioners' sugar

5 cups Rice Chex cereal

½ cup dairy-free semisweet chocolate chips

¼ cup peanut butter

4 tablespoons nondairy butter

1 teaspoon vanilla extract

1 cup salted roasted cashew pieces

1 cup salted roasted almonds

1. Line a baking sheet with parchment paper. Put the sugar in a zip-top bag. Place the cereal in a large bowl.

2. In a small saucepan, combine the chocolate chips, peanut butter, butter, and vanilla and stir over low heat until melted. Drizzle over the cereal. With a spatula, carefully toss to coat the cereal well.

3. Transfer the coated cereal to the bag with the sugar, seal, and shake it to coat. Add the nuts, reseal the bag, and shake it to coat.

4. Pour the mixture onto the prepared baking sheet to cool. Store in an airtight glass container for up to 1 week.

RECIPE TIP: This snack is best stored in a glass container to prevent it from getting crushed.

Per Serving (½ cup) Calories: 330; Protein: 7g; Total carbohydrates: 32g; Sugars: 8g; Fiber: 3g; Total fat: 20g; Saturated fat: 4g; Cholesterol: 0mg; Sodium: 186mg

Desserts and Treats

Cheesecake with Mixed Berry Topping, page 150

Chocolate Angel Food Cake

TREE NUT-FREE, PEANUT-FREE, SOY-FREE, VEGETARIAN

Angel food cake is a delicate fat-free cake that usually hits stores in the summertime and for Labor Day weekend celebrations. It's an ultra-fluffy cake made by folding flour into egg whites beaten to stiff, glossy peaks. This recipe incorporates cocoa powder for a little extra indulgence and is great for chocolate lovers who want a dessert on the lighter side. It's delicious served with nondairy whipped cream or whipped topping and fresh berries.

- **Prep time: 30 minutes**
- **Cook time: 45 minutes**
- **Serves 12**

1½ cups sugar, divided

¼ cup all-purpose gluten-free flour

½ cup unsweetened cocoa powder

½ cup potato starch

¼ cup tapioca flour

2 teaspoons xanthan gum

12 large egg whites, at room temperature

1½ teaspoons vanilla extract

½ teaspoon salt (preferably pink Himalayan)

1 teaspoon cream of tartar

1. Preheat the oven to 325°F. Do not grease an angel food cake pan.

2. Sift ¾ cup of sugar, the flour, cocoa powder, potato starch, tapioca flour, and xanthan gum into a medium bowl.

3. In a large bowl, with an electric mixer, beat the egg whites, vanilla, and salt on medium-high speed until foamy. Add the cream of tartar and beat until soft peaks form. Continue beating while gradually adding the remaining ¾ cup of sugar, ¼ cup at a time, until incorporated. Continue to beat until stiff, glossy peaks form.

4. Sift the flour mixture, one-third at a time, over the egg whites, carefully folding with a spatula after each addition until all the ingredients are incorporated.

5. Pour the batter into the pan. Run a knife through the center of the batter to release any air bubbles. Smooth the top with a spatula for even baking. Bake for 40 to 45 minutes, or until the top is lightly browned and cracked and a toothpick inserted in the center comes out with just a few crumbs.

6. Place the cake pan upside down on a wire rack, over the neck of a tall wine bottle, or on the feet of the pan (if the pan has feet) and let cool completely for 2 hours. Run a knife carefully around the edges of the pan to loosen the cake, then flip the cake onto a wire rack.

INGREDIENT TIP: Make sure to sift the flour and cocoa first so there are no clumps in the batter.

Per Serving Calories: 159; Protein: 5g; Total carbohydrates: 36g; Sugars: 25g; Fiber: 3g; Total fat: 1g; Saturated fat: 0g; Cholesterol: 0mg; Sodium: 155mg

Fudgy Avocado–Chocolate Pudding

EGG-FREE, PEANUT-FREE, SOY-FREE, VEGAN

If you love to indulge in rich chocolate pudding, then you will love this ultra-fudgy recipe. Not only is it dairy-free, this decadent dessert boasts loads of healthy omega-3 fats and antioxidant-rich chocolate to boost brain power!

- **Prep time: 15 minutes, plus 1 hour to chill**
- **Serves 6**

1 cup dairy-free chocolate chips or chocolate chunks

3 cups diced avocado (about 3 very large avocados)

⅓ cup maple syrup

¼ cup nondairy milk, such as almond milk, cashew milk, or coconut milk

⅓ cup unsweetened cocoa powder

2 teaspoons vanilla extract

⅛ teaspoon salt (preferably pink Himalayan)

Nondairy whipped cream (optional), for topping

1. In a small microwave-safe bowl, microwave the chocolate chips in 30-second increments, stirring well after each, until smooth and melted.

2. In a food processor, combine the avocado, maple syrup, milk, cocoa powder, vanilla, salt, and melted chocolate. Blend until smooth.

3. Divide the pudding into six small bowls. Cover and refrigerate for at least 1 hour and up to 2 days. Top with whipped cream (if using) right before serving.

SUBSTITUTION TIP: You can swap vegan white chocolate for the chocolate chips for a richer, creamier (almost dairy-like) flavor.

Per Serving (without whipped cream)
Calories: 397; Protein: 6g; Total carbohydrates: 49g; Sugars: 11g; Fiber: 8g; Total fat: 6g; Saturated fat: 9g; Cholesterol: 0mg; Sodium: 65mg

Chewy Double Chocolate Chip Cookies

PEANUT-FREE, SOY-FREE, VEGETARIAN

I do not think I have ever met anyone who doesn't like a chocolate chip cookie. Adding coconut milk powder and decadent chocolate morsels to the dough makes these cookies incredibly chewy and mouthwateringly delicious! Make sure to bake just until slightly glossy so they stay chewy inside and not overbaked or crisp on the outside.

- **Prep time: 10 minutes, plus 1 hour to chill**
- **Cook time: 8 minutes**
- **Makes 36 cookies**

8 tablespoons nondairy butter, melted

½ cup packed dark brown sugar

⅓ cup coconut sugar

1 large egg

1 teaspoon vanilla extract

½ teaspoon salt (preferably pink Himalayan)

½ teaspoon baking soda

¾ cup all-purpose gluten-free flour

½ cup unsweetened cocoa powder

¾ cup coconut milk powder

2 cups dairy-free chocolate chips

1. In a large bowl, combine the melted butter, brown sugar, and coconut sugar. With an electric mixer on low speed, beat until blended. Add the egg and vanilla and beat on low until creamed.

2. Sift together the salt, baking soda, flour, cocoa powder, and coconut milk powder. Slowly add to the wet mixture and beat until well blended and a dough forms. Stir in the chocolate chips. Cover the bowl and refrigerate for 1 hour or overnight.

3. Preheat the oven to 350°F. Line a baking sheet with parchment paper.

4. With a 1-inch cookie scoop, drop the dough onto the pan and roll it into a ball. Repeat with the remaining dough.

5. Working in batches, bake for 8 minutes, or until slightly glossy. Let cool on the pan for about 5 minutes, then transfer to a wire rack to cool completely. Store in an airtight container for up to 3 days or in the refrigerator for 5 days.

INGREDIENT TIP: Coconut milk powder can be found at most natural foods stores or online. It tends to clump, so it is important to sift the dry ingredients together so they incorporate into a smooth batter.

Per Serving (1 cookie) Calories: 134; Protein: 2g; Total carbohydrates: 17g; Sugars: 4g; Fiber: 1g; Total fat: 8g; Saturated fat: 4g; Cholesterol: 5mg; Sodium: 73mg

Chocolate Date Truffles

EGG-FREE, PEANUT-FREE, SOY-FREE, VEGAN

These raw vegan chocolate truffles have a creamy filling thanks to coconut milk powder, dates, and cashews. They are much healthier, but do not skimp on flavor! The truffles are simply rolled in a cocoa sugar coating (which has fewer calories and less fat).

- **Prep time: 40 minutes, plus 1 hour to soak and 1 hour to freeze**

- **Makes 12 truffles**

FOR THE TRUFFLES

1 cup cashews

1 cup pitted dates

1 cup filtered water

½ cup coconut milk powder

½ cup unsweetened cocoa powder

¼ cup coconut flour

1 teaspoon vanilla extract

FOR THE COCOA SUGAR COATING

3 tablespoons confectioners' sugar

3 tablespoons unsweetened cocoa powder

TO MAKE THE TRUFFLES

1. Soak the cashews and dates in the filtered water for 1 hour.

2. Drain the cashews and dates, transfer to a food processor, and pulse until smooth.

3. In a large bowl, stir together the coconut milk powder, cocoa powder, coconut flour, and vanilla. Stir in the cashew and date mixture until combined. Cover and refrigerate for about 30 minutes.

4. Line a baking sheet with parchment paper. Roll the truffle mixture into 12 balls and place on the prepared baking sheet. Set the pan in the freezer for 1 hour to harden.

TO MAKE THE COCOA SUGAR COATING

In a small bowl, stir together the confectioners' sugar and cocoa powder. One at a time, roll 6 of the truffles in the mixture and return to the baking sheet.

VARIATION TIP: To coat all the truffles in chocolate, in a small microwave-safe bowl, microwave 2 cups chocolate chips in 30-second increments, stirring well after each, until smooth and melted. One at a time, roll the truffles in the melted chocolate and return to the pan. Sprinkle with a few coarse salt crystals, if desired. Store in the refrigerator in an airtight container.

Per Serving Calories: 177; Protein: 4g; Total carbohydrates: 23g; Sugars: 12g; Fiber: 4g; Total fat: 10g; Saturated fat: 4g; Cholesterol: 0mg; Sodium: 13mg

Lemon Cookies with Lemon Icing

EGG-FREE, TREE NUT-FREE, PEANUT-FREE, SOY-FREE, VEGAN

Every holiday, my younger son asks to make these classic cut-out lemon cookies, which are flavored with lemon zest and a splash of lemon extract. He had them once at our town's local Christmas festival and has been hooked ever since. The recipe calls for them to be cut into 3-inch rounds, but you can use any shape you'd like.

- **Prep time: 20 minutes, plus 30 minutes to chill**
- **Cook time: 8 minutes**
- **Makes 16 cookies**

FOR THE COOKIES

½ cup maple syrup

4 tablespoons nondairy butter, softened

2 teaspoons grated lemon zest

½ teaspoon lemon extract

1 cup all-purpose gluten-free flour

⅓ cup tapioca flour

1¼ teaspoons baking powder

¼ teaspoon salt (preferably pink Himalayan)

FOR THE ICING

1 cup confectioners' sugar

1½ to 2 tablespoons warm water

½ teaspoon lemon extract

TO MAKE THE COOKIES

1. Preheat the oven to 350°F. Line 2 baking sheets with silicone baking mats or parchment paper.

2. In a large bowl, combine the maple syrup, butter, lemon zest, and lemon extract. Stir in the gluten-free flour, tapioca flour, baking powder, and salt until it forms a dough. Wrap the dough in parchment paper or wax paper and refrigerate for 30 minutes.

3. Generously dust a piece of wax paper with tapioca flour. Add the dough, dust the top with more tapioca flour, and roll the dough between 2 pieces of wax paper to about ¼ inch thick. Using a 3-inch round cookie cutter, cut the dough into rounds. Divide the cookies between the 2 prepared baking sheets and bake for 8 minutes, or until lightly browned. Let cool for 3 minutes on the pan, then transfer to a rack to cool completely.

TO MAKE THE ICING

Once the cookies have cooled, in a large bowl, with an electric mixer, beat the sugar, water, and lemon extract on medium speed for 2 minutes. Pipe or spread the icing over the cookies.

VARIATION TIP: Turn these into yummy sandwich cookies by spreading the icing on the top of one cookie and placing another cookie on top.

Per Serving (1 cookie) Calories: 130; Protein: 1g; Total carbohydrates: 24g; Sugars: 6g; Fiber: 0g; Total fat: 4g; Saturated fat: 1g; Cholesterol: 0mg; Sodium: 37mg

Cheesecake with Mixed Berry Topping

EGG-FREE, PEANUT-FREE, SOY-FREE, VEGETARIAN

Sweet, rich cheesecake happens to be one of my husband's favorite desserts, but he has an allergic reaction when he consumes dairy products. But just because you can't have dairy shouldn't mean you have to miss out on cheesecake! And not the kind using vegan cream cheese as a "filler." This one is created with a creamy filling and a no-bake date and nut crust for a sweet blend that simply melts in your mouth. It also involves zero baking. It's a favorite dessert for the Fourth of July and during the summer months.

- **Prep time: 2 hours 15 minutes**
- **Cook time: 10 minutes**
- **Serves 8**

FOR THE CRUST

6 tablespoons nondairy butter

1 cup gluten-free rolled oats

1 cup tapioca flour

1 cup dry unsweetened coconut

6 tablespoons maple syrup

Pinch of salt (preferably pink Himalayan)

FOR THE FILLING AND TOPPING

½ teaspoon salt (preferably pink Himalayan)

½ cup water

1½ teaspoons unflavored vegetarian gelatin

16 ounces nondairy cream cheese

½ cup canned coconut milk, full fat, separated

1 tablespoon nutritional yeast

1 teaspoon vanilla extract

⅔ cup plus 2 tablespoons honey, divided

1½ cups mixed berries (strawberries, blueberries, raspberries, blackberries)

TO MAKE THE CRUST

1. Preheat the oven to 350°F. Line a 9-inch springform cake pan with parchment paper.

2. In a food processor, place the butter, oats, tapioca flour, coconut, maple syrup, and salt. Pulse just until it resembles a fine crumb dough.

3. Using your hands, press the mixture onto the base of the springform pan. Place in the oven and bake 10 minutes while preparing the filling. Set aside.

TO MAKE THE FILLING

1. In a small saucepan, combine the salt and water and sprinkle with gelatin. Over medium-high heat, bring to a boil, stirring, for 2 minutes, or until the gelatin dissolves. Set aside to cool.

2. In a large bowl with an electric mixer, beat the cream cheese, coconut milk, nutritional yeast, vanilla, and ⅔ cup of the honey. Slowly pour in the gelatin mixture and beat on low until blended.

3. Pour the mixture into the prepared crust and refrigerate for 2 hours or until firm.

4. To serve, place the cheesecake on a cake plate. Top with the berries and drizzle with the remaining 2 tablespoons of honey.

SIMPLIFY IT: To keep everything from sticking, line the pan! To cut parchment paper in a round to fit the pan, place the removable pan bottom on the paper and trace around it, then cut inside the line so it is still smaller and will fit inside.

Per Serving Calories: 569; Protein: 7g; Total carbohydrates: 66g; Sugars: 39g; Fiber: 7g; Total fat: 33g; Saturated fat: 13g; Cholesterol: 0mg; Sodium: 373mg

Pecan Pie with Cashew Crust

PEANUT-FREE, SOY-FREE, VEGETARIAN

Nothing satisfies a sweet tooth like a pie made almost entirely of sugar! That's exactly what a pecan pie is—it naturally melts in your mouth at first bite. Instead of adding the filling to a basic pie crust, this grain-free version uses cashews blended with almond meal for the crust. The nutty flavors complement the rich, sugary filling and crunchy pecans. This pie is always a hit at holiday parties.

- **Prep time: 15 minutes**
- **Cook time: 50 minutes**
- **Serves 8**

FOR THE CRUST

1½ cups almond meal

6 tablespoons coconut oil, melted

1½ cups cashews

1 large egg

1 large egg white

1 teaspoon vanilla extract

1 tablespoon coconut sugar

FOR THE FILLING

3 tablespoons nondairy butter

¾ cup dark corn syrup

3 large eggs

¼ cup coconut sugar

2 teaspoons vanilla extract

1 teaspoon grated orange zest

¼ teaspoon salt (preferably pink Himalayan)

2 cups pecan halves

TO MAKE THE CRUST

1. Preheat the oven to 350°F. Coat a 9-inch pie dish with nonstick cooking spray.

2. In a food processor, combine the almond meal, oil, cashews, whole egg, egg white, vanilla, and coconut sugar. Blend for about 30 seconds, or until well blended and smooth.

3. Transfer to the pie dish. With your hands, evenly press the mixture onto the bottom and up the sides. With a fork, poke holes in the crust about three times in a circle. Bake for 10 minutes. Place on a rack to cool slightly. Leave the oven on.

TO MAKE THE FILLING

1. In a medium saucepan, melt the butter over medium heat. Add the corn syrup, eggs, coconut sugar, vanilla, orange zest, and salt. Bring to a boil, whisking constantly. Boil for 1 minute, or until the mixture is smooth and silky. Remove from the heat.

2. Arrange the pecans on the bottom of the pie crust. Pour the egg mixture over the pecans. Return the pie to the oven and bake for 40 minutes, or until the filling is set. Let cool to room temperature. Store any leftover pie in the refrigerator.

RECIPE TIP: When adding the eggs to the filling, quickly and thoroughly whisk the eggs so they cook evenly and don't scramble.

Per Serving Calories: 733; Protein: 15g; Total carbohydrates: 45g; Sugars: 17g; Fiber: 6g; Total fat: 57g; Saturated fat: 15g; Cholesterol: 93mg; Sodium: 123mg

Upside-Down Pear Cake

PEANUT-FREE, SOY-FREE, VEGETARIAN

This tasty spiced cake has comforting notes of cinnamon and brown sugar caramelized around pears and finished off with a drizzle of honey. It's one of our favorite desserts during the holidays. Pureed pear and chunks of pears throughout the batter help bring out unique flavors and texture. It can also be made with just apples or a combination of apples and pears.

- **Prep time: 25 minutes**
- **Cook time: 45 minutes**
- **Serves 12**

4 pears, peeled, halved, and cored, divided

½ cup nondairy milk

2 large eggs

1 teaspoon vanilla extract

4 tablespoons honey, divided

1 cup all-purpose gluten-free flour

½ cup almond meal

½ cup coconut sugar

2 teaspoons ground cinnamon

2 teaspoons baking powder

½ teaspoon baking soda

¼ teaspoon salt (preferably pink Himalayan)

1. Preheat the oven to 350°F. Coat a 9-inch cake pan with nonstick cooking spray.

2. In a food processor, combine 1 pear, the milk, eggs, vanilla, and 2 tablespoons of honey. Process until smooth.

3. In a large bowl, combine the flour, almond meal, coconut sugar, cinnamon, baking powder, baking soda, and salt. Stir in the milk mixture just until combined.

4. Slice the remaining pears and arrange in a fan pattern on the bottom of the cake pan. Pour the batter on top of the pears.

5. Bake for 45 minutes, or until a toothpick inserted in the center comes out clean. Let it cool in the pan on a rack for 15 minutes.

6. Using a knife, loosen the edges of the cake. Turn onto a wire rack to finish cooling. Place on a serving plate and drizzle with the remaining 2 tablespoons of honey.

RECIPE TIP: Be careful when flipping the cake over that it does not fall apart. Place the wire rack directly on top of the cake pan and flip while holding the pan and rack together. Give it a couple of taps all around to release the cake.

Per Serving Calories: 177; Protein: 4g; Total carbohydrates: 34g; Sugars: 21g; Fiber: 3g; Total fat: 4g; Saturated fat: 0g; Cholesterol: 27mg; Sodium: 122mg

Mini Honey Tea Cakes

PEANUT-FREE, SOY-FREE, VEGETARIAN

In England, it's essential to shut everything down in the afternoon and have a tea break. I remember visiting Heathrow when I was 16 and that is just what we did. We even went to a quaint little teahouse where we were served pastries with our tea. These mini honey-flavored cakes make the perfect delicate treat for an afternoon party or brunch. They can be eaten alone or frosted with Lemon Icing (page 149).

- **Prep time: 10 minutes**
- **Cook time: 15 minutes**
- **Makes 32 mini cakes**

1 cup almond meal

½ cup potato starch

¼ cup coconut flour

1 teaspoon xanthan gum

1 teaspoon baking powder

½ teaspoon baking soda

½ teaspoon salt (preferably pink Himalayan)

2 large eggs

¾ cup nondairy yogurt

¾ cup honey

1 teaspoon vanilla extract

Lemon Icing (optional, page 149)

1. Preheat the oven to 350°F. Coat a 24-cup mini muffin pan with nonstick cooking spray.

2. In a large bowl, sift together the almond meal, potato starch, coconut flour, xanthan gum, baking powder, baking soda, and salt.

3. In a small bowl, whisk together the eggs, yogurt, honey, and vanilla. Stir into the flour mixture just until combined. Fill the 24 mini muffin cups, reserving the remaining batter for a second batch.

4. Bake for 13 to 15 minutes, or until the tops are slightly golden brown. Let cool 5 minutes in the pan, then transfer to a wire rack to cool completely.

5. For the second batch, let the pan cool, then coat 8 of the cups with nonstick cooking spray and divide the batter equally among the cups. Fill each empty cup with 2 table-spoons of water. Bake as before and let cool.

6. Once cooled, spread with lemon icing (if using).

SUBSTITUTION TIP: If you cannot consume xanthan gum or any gums, use 2 tablespoons psyllium husk instead.

Per Serving (1 mini cake) Calories: 65; Protein: 1g; Total carbohydrates: 10g; Sugars: 7g; Fiber: 1g; Total fat: 2g; Saturated fat: 0g; Cholesterol: 12mg; Sodium: 64mg

Homemade Fudge Pops

EGG-FREE, PEANUT-FREE, SOY-FREE, VEGETARIAN

Whenever a chocolate craving hits, these pops are always on my list of indulgences. They're so easy to make at home and much healthier than store-bought ones, which are loaded with white sugar, dairy, and other processed ingredients. The secret to the great texture of these bars is the gelatin, which helps make them cream-like. They go fast, so you may just want to double up on the recipe!

- **Prep time: 10 minutes, plus 4 hours to freeze**
- **Cook time: 5 minutes**
- **Makes 6 pops**

1 (13.5-ounce) can full-fat coconut milk, divided

1½ teaspoons unflavored vegan gelatin

½ cup honey

⅓ cup unsweetened cocoa powder

2 teaspoons vanilla extract

1. Shake the can of coconut milk to blend contents. Pour ½ cup of the coconut milk into a small saucepan and sprinkle with the gelatin. Bring to a boil over medium heat and boil for 2 minutes, stirring, or until the gelatin dissolves. Set aside to cool slightly.

2. In a blender, combine the remaining coconut milk, the gelatin mixture, honey, cocoa powder, and vanilla. Blend until smooth. Pour into 6 ice pop molds. Freeze for 4 hours before serving.

Per Serving (1 pop) Calories: 225; Protein: 2g; Total carbohydrates: 28g; Sugars: 24g; Fiber: 2g; Total fat: 14g; Saturated fat: 12g; Cholesterol: 0mg; Sodium: 10mg

Essential Extras

Clockwise from left: Creamy Dill Dressing, page 167; Butternut Squash Sauce, page 163; Homemade Ketchup, page 164; Almond Turmeric Dressing, page 168; Green Goddess Dressing, page 169

Easy Fresh Salsa

EGG-FREE, TREE NUT-FREE, PEANUT-FREE, SOY-FREE, VEGAN

Juicy fresh red tomatoes, jalapeño pepper, and lime juice come together for a quick and spicy salsa fresca. This healthy appetizer or sauce is ready in just 5 minutes! If you prefer milder heat, skip the jalapeño. For maximum flavor, make it at the peak of tomato season. This salsa is great to serve over tacos or burritos, or with chips or nachos.

- **Prep time: 5 minutes**
- **Serves 4**

7 large vine or Roma or plum tomatoes, cored and quartered

1 large garlic clove

½ shallot, peeled

1 jalapeño, halved and seeded

1 poblano pepper, halved and seeded

1 cup packed fresh cilantro leaves

Juice of 1 lime

½ teaspoon salt (preferably pink Himalayan)

¼ teaspoon chili powder

1. In a food processor, combine the tomatoes, garlic, shallot, jalapeño, poblano, cilantro, lime juice, salt, and chili powder. Pulse at a low speed in 1-second intervals 5 to 10 times, or until the desired consistency is achieved.

2. Transfer to a serving bowl if serving immediately. Or transfer to an airtight container and refrigerate for up to 1 week.

VARIATION TIP: Turn this into salsa verde by using tomatillos in place of the tomatoes. For either version, make it a roasted salsa by roasting the tomatoes or tomatillos on a rimmed baking sheet at 400°F for 20 to 30 minutes, or until browned, and let cool completely before making the salsa.

Per Serving Calories: 63; Protein: 3g; Total carbohydrates: 14g; Sugars: 9g; Fiber: 4g; Total fat: 1g; Saturated fat: 0g; Cholesterol: 0mg; Sodium: 310mg

Cashew Milk

EGG-FREE, PEANUT-FREE, SOY-FREE, VEGAN

Cashews are naturally creamy and you can make this milk effortlessly in the blender. If using a high-powered blender, straining the nuts may not be needed since they're blended to a smooth finish. Making homemade nut milk is super easy and much healthier than store-bought since there are no additives or preservatives. Use it in baked goods, latte beverages, over homemade granola, and in any recipe that calls for milk.

- **Prep time: 10 minutes, plus 3 hours to soak**
- **Makes 4 cups**

1 cup cashews, raw and unsalted

6 cups filtered water, divided

1 teaspoon vanilla extract

3 pitted dates

Pinch of salt (preferably pink Himalayan)

1. Soak the cashews in 2 cups filtered water in the refrigerator for 3 hours. Drain and rinse under cold water.

2. In a blender, combine the cashews, the remaining 4 cups of filtered water, the vanilla, dates and salt. Blend on high until well blended.

3. Using a nut bag or cheesecloth, place the bag over a large bowl. Pour the blended cashew mix into the bag. Give the bag a good squeeze to push the nut milk into the bowl. Save the remaining cashew "meat" to add to muffins and baked goods.

4. Transfer the milk to a pitcher with a lid and refrigerate for up to 5 days.

INGREDIENT TIP: If time permits, soak the nuts overnight to remove enzymes (which will support easier digestion).

VARIATION TIPS: Substitute 1 tablespoon of honey or maple syrup for the dates. Or to make this milk for soups and savory dishes, leave out the dates and vanilla. You can also follow this recipe using almonds to make almond milk.

Per Serving (1 cup) Calories: 60; Protein: 0g; Total carbohydrates: 9 g; Sugars: 7g; Fiber: 0g; Total fat: 3g; Saturated fat: 0g; Cholesterol: 0mg; Sodium: 170mg

Chocolate Ganache

EGG-FREE, PEANUT-FREE, SOY-FREE, VEGAN

This ganache is wonderful drizzled over cake or brownies, or as a filling for cupcakes. It's a simple, creamy, soft mixture of dairy-free chocolate and coconut cream that's so good you might just want to eat it by the spoonful! Add a tablespoon to punch up hot chocolate, or drizzle over the Mini Honey Tea Cakes (page 155).

- **Prep time: 5 minutes**
- **Cook time: 2 minutes**
- **Makes about 1½ cups**

1 cup dairy-free dark chocolate chips

1 cup canned coconut cream

1 teaspoon vanilla extract

1. Place the chocolate chips in a heat-proof medium bowl.

2. In a small saucepan, heat the coconut cream until it is just about to boil. Pour over the chips and whisk together until melted. Whisk in the vanilla until very smooth and creamy.

3. Store in an airtight container in the refrigerator for up to 1 week.

INGREDIENT TIP: Before measuring the coconut cream for this, pour the whole can into a small saucepan and melt over low heat so the fat is evenly distributed. Then measure out the cup that you need here. Store the rest of the coconut cream in an airtight container in the refrigerator for another use.

SUBSTITUTION TIP: Canned coconut milk (full-fat) can also be used in place of coconut cream.

Per Serving (2 tablespoons) Calories: 148; Protein: 1g; Total carbohydrates: 13g; Sugars: 10g; Fiber: 1g; Total fat: 11g; Saturated fat: 8g; Cholesterol: 0mg; Sodium: 7mg

Butternut Squash Cream Sauce

EGG-FREE, PEANUT-FREE, SOY-FREE, VEGAN

This earthy sauce is a great way to still enjoy dishes such as mac and cheese, lasagna, and pizza. Not only good for dairy-free folks, it makes a great alternative for people with a tomato allergy who cannot use red sauce. Roasting the vegetables first caramelizes them, bringing out their natural sweetness.

- **Prep time: 20 minutes**
- **Cook time: 35 minutes**
- **Serves 4**

1 (3½-pound) butternut squash, peeled, seeded, and cut into cubes

1 tablespoon extra-virgin olive oil

1 small onion

2 garlic cloves

½ to ¾ cup cashew milk or coconut milk beverage

¼ cup nutritional yeast

2 tablespoons nondairy butter

1 tablespoon Dijon mustard

¾ teaspoon salt (preferably pink Himalayan)

¼ teaspoon freshly ground black pepper

1. Preheat the oven to 400°F.

2. Place the butternut squash on a large rimmed baking sheet and drizzle with the oil, tossing to coat. Add a drizzle of water to the pan. Wrap the onion and garlic cloves in aluminum foil and add to the pan. Roast for 35 minutes, or until browned and tender. Remove from the oven and let cool slightly.

3. In a blender, combine the squash, onion, garlic, ½ cup of milk, the nutritional yeast, butter, mustard, salt, and pepper. Blend until smooth and creamy. If needed for a thinner consistency, gradually add up to ¼ cup more milk.

SIMPLIFY IT: To save loads of time peeling and slicing, purchase pre-cut butternut squash.

Per Serving Calories: 234; Protein: 9g; Total carbohydrates: 33g; Sugars: 7g; Fiber: 9g; Total fat: 10g; Saturated fat: 2g; Cholesterol: 0mg; Sodium: 619mg

Homemade Ketchup

EGG-FREE, TREE NUT-FREE, PEANUT-FREE, SOY-FREE

A thick and rich condiment—with no high-fructose corn syrup—made with honey, spices, vinegar, and sweet tomatoes. This ketchup will keep for 3 weeks in the refrigerator. Use it on burgers, as a dip with fries, on meatloaf, or as a key ingredient in Barbecue Sauce (page 165).

- **Prep time: 10 minutes**
- **Cook time: 40 minutes**
- **Makes 2 cups**

1 (29-ounce) can tomato puree

½ cup apple cider vinegar

⅓ cup honey

2 tablespoons tomato paste

⅛ teaspoon onion powder

⅛ teaspoon garlic powder

½ teaspoon salt (preferably pink Himalayan)

2 sticks cinnamon

15 whole cloves

1 whole nutmeg

2 bay leaves

2 tablespoons corn starch

1. In a large saucepan, combine the tomato puree, vinegar, honey, tomato paste, onion powder, garlic powder, and salt. Tie the cinnamon, cloves, nutmeg, and bay leaves in a square of cheesecloth and add to the pan.

2. Bring to a simmer over medium-high heat. Reduce the heat to low and simmer for 20 minutes, stirring occasionally.

3. Remove the cheesecloth bundle. Let the mixture simmer for 20 to 30 minutes and stir in cornstarch. Let simmer until the desired thickness is achieved.

4. Cool completely, then transfer to an airtight glass container and store in the refrigerator for up to 3 weeks.

Per Serving Calories: 44; Protein: 1g; Total carbohydrates: 12g; Sugars: 8g; Fiber: 1g; Total fat: <1g; Saturated fat: 0g; Cholesterol: 0mg; Sodium: 309mg

Barbecue Sauce

EGG-FREE, PEANUT-FREE, SOY-FREE

Use this easy, smoky, gluten-free barbecue sauce as a marinade, dressing, or dip! Most store-bought brands sneak in small amounts of gluten to thicken the sauce. This recipe uses lots of ingredients, but it's simple to make and packed full of flavor with smoky notes. We love it on vegetables or ribs, for grilling or slow cooking, as a sauce on pizza, or brushed onto meatloaf or roasts.

- **Prep time: 15 minutes**
- **Cook time: 10 minutes**
- **Makes about 2¾ cups**

2 cups gluten-free ketchup, store-bought or homemade (page 164)

¼ cup apple cider vinegar

¼ cup freshly squeezed lemon juice

¼ cup molasses

¼ cup water

¼ cup coconut sugar

2 tablespoons coconut aminos or gluten-free soy sauce

1 tablespoon natural liquid smoke

1 tablespoon mustard powder

½ teaspoon freshly ground black pepper

¼ teaspoon ground ginger

¼ teaspoon onion powder

¼ teaspoon ground allspice

1. In a medium saucepan, combine the ketchup, vinegar, lemon juice, molasses, water, coconut sugar, coconut aminos, liquid smoke, mustard powder, pepper, ginger, onion powder, and allspice. Bring to a boil over high heat. Reduce the heat to low and simmer, stirring occasionally, for 5 minutes, or until it starts to thicken.

2. Remove from the heat and let it cool for 10 minutes before using. Or cool completely, transfer to an airtight container, and store in the refrigerator for up to 1 week.

INGREDIENT TIP: This recipe gets loads of flavor from liquid smoke. It only calls for 1 tablespoon, as a little goes a long way, so don't add more without tasting first.

Per Serving (2 tablespoons) Calories: 44; Protein: 1g; Total carbohydrates: 11g; Sugars: 9g; Fiber: 0g; Total fat: 0g; Saturated fat: 0g; Cholesterol: 0mg; Sodium: 245mg

Vegan Ricotta Cheese

EGG-FREE, PEANUT-FREE, SOY-FREE, VEGAN

This "cheese" is made with raw cashews or blanched almonds and has a mild ricotta-like flavor and consistency. It's a game changer for a dairy-free lifestyle. Use it as a dip with chips and vegetables, mixed into pasta with tomato sauce, or add to lasagna or baked pasta.

- **Prep time: 2 hours**
- **Makes about 2 cups**

2 cups raw unsalted cashews or blanched almonds

3 cups filtered water, divided

1 tablespoon freshly squeezed lemon juice

2 teaspoons nutritional yeast

2 teaspoons distilled white vinegar

1 teaspoon salt (preferably pink Himalayan)

1. In a large bowl, soak the cashews in 2 cups of water in the refrigerator for to 2 hours to soften. Drain and rinse under cold water.

2. In a blender, combine the cashews, lemon juice, nutritional yeast, vinegar, salt, and remaining 1 cup of water. Blend until smooth.

3. Line a large sieve with cheesecloth (you can set the sieve in the sink or over a bowl). Pour the blended cashew mixture into the sieve. Twist the cheesecloth closed and give it a good squeeze to remove liquid (which should be discarded). Depending on how thick you want your ricotta, you can squeeze out more or less liquid.

4. Scrape the ricotta cheese out of the cheesecloth into an airtight container and store in the refrigerator for up to 5 days.

SIMPLIFY IT: I prefer to use a nut bag as opposed to cheesecloth. It's reusable and can be found online. Plus, it doesn't allow pieces of thread to slip into the food.

Per Serving Calories: 199; Protein: 6g; Total carbohydrates: 12g; Sugars: 2g; Fiber: 1g; Total fat: 16g; Saturated fat: 3g; Cholesterol: 0mg; Sodium: 297mg

Creamy Dill Dressing

EGG-FREE, TREE NUT-FREE, PEANUT-FREE, SOY-FREE, VEGAN

A flavorful herb dressing packed with lemon, dill, and mint. It's a wonderful addition to summer salads, steamed beets, baked salmon, or pork; it's also delicious served as a sandwich spread or a dip with veggie sticks or potato chips.

- **Prep time: 5 minutes**
- **Makes 1½ cups**

1 large bunch fresh dill, stems included

1 large bunch fresh mint, stems included

1 shallot, peeled

1 cup nondairy yogurt

½ cup water

Juice of 1 lemon

½ teaspoon salt (preferably pink Himalayan)

¼ teaspoon freshly ground black pepper

In a blender or food processor, combine the dill, mint, shallot, yogurt, water, lemon juice, salt, and pepper. Process until well blended. Store in an airtight container in the refrigerator for up to 5 days.

RECIPE TIP: Adding the stems and leaves of the herbs eliminates wasted ingredients and boosts flavor. When processing, pulse lightly for a chunkier dressing or longer until the herbs are blended smooth, depending on your preference.

Per Serving (2 tablespoons) Calories: 29; Protein: 1g; Total carbohydrates: 5g; Sugars: 1g; Fiber: 1g; Total fat: 1g; Saturated fat: 0g; Cholesterol: 0mg; Sodium: 109mg

Almond Turmeric Dressing

EGG-FREE, PEANUT-FREE, SOY-FREE, VEGAN

A healthy, zesty blend of turmeric, lemon, and almonds. Just puree all the dressing ingredients in a food processor until smooth. It's packed with healthy anti-inflammatory and cancer-fighting ingredients. Serve over salad or use as a marinade for salmon or chicken.

- **Prep time: 5 minutes, plus 1 hour to soak**
- **Makes about 1 cup**

½ cup slivered almonds

1 cup filtered water, divided

1 garlic clove

2 teaspoons grated lemon zest

Juice of 1 lemon

1 tablespoon maple syrup

1 teaspoon ground turmeric

¼ teaspoon salt (preferably pink Himalayan)

⅛ teaspoon freshly ground black pepper

1. Soak the almonds in ½ cup of water for 1 hour. Drain and rinse under cold water.

2. In a food processor, combine the almonds, remaining ½ cup of water, the garlic, lemon zest, lemon juice, maple syrup, turmeric, salt, and pepper. Process until smooth. Store in the refrigerator for up to 1 week.

RECIPE TIP: Adding fresh lemon zest to the dressing complements the turmeric by tempering its flavor and giving the dressing a reviving punch.

Per Serving (2 tablespoons) Calories: 44; Protein: 1g; Total carbohydrates: 4g; Sugars: 2g; Fiber: 1g; Total fat: 3g; Saturated fat: 0g; Cholesterol: 0mg; Sodium: 75mg

Green Goddess Dressing

EGG-FREE, TREE NUT-FREE, PEANUT-FREE, SOY-FREE, VEGAN

Unfortunately, most store-bought salad dressings, sauces, and dips have added dairy as well as preservatives and ingredients that don't benefit our bodies. This dressing takes about 5 minutes to make and contains 100 percent fresh ingredients. It's packed with vegetables, basil, parsley, chives, lemon, onion, and garlic. It's fabulous on just about anything.

- **Prep time: 5 minutes**
- **Makes about 1 cup**

1 avocado, cut into chunks

¼ onion

2 scallions, roots trimmed, cut into several pieces

1 garlic clove

1 large bunch fresh parsley

1 large bunch fresh basil

1 tablespoon chopped fresh chives

¾ cup water

¼ teaspoon grated lemon zest

Juice of 1 lemon

2 tablespoons extra-virgin olive oil

1 teaspoon apple cider vinegar

1 teaspoon salt (preferably pink Himalayan)

⅛ teaspoon freshly ground black pepper

In a blender or food processor, combine the avocado, onion, scallions, garlic, parsley, basil, chives, water, lemon zest, lemon juice, oil, vinegar, salt, and pepper. Blend until the desired consistency is achieved. Blending for 30 seconds will provide a chunkier dressing; blend longer for a smooth dressing. Store in the refrigerator for up to 3 days.

INGREDIENT TIP: To tell if an avocado is ripe, lay it in the palm of your hand and squeeze gently. It should feel soft and slightly tender, but not squishy or mushy. Once sliced open, if it has brown spots, select another one as it will have a slightly rancid taste.

Per Serving Calories: 77; Protein: 1g; Total carbohydrates: 4g; Sugars: 1g; Fiber: 2g; Total fat: 7g; Saturated fat: 1g; Cholesterol: 0mg; Sodium: 298mg

Measurement Conversions

	US STANDARD	US STANDARD (OUNCES)	METRIC (APPROXIMATE)
VOLUME EQUIVALENTS (LIQUID)	2 tablespoons	1 fl. oz.	30 mL
	¼ cup	2 fl. oz.	60 mL
	½ cup	4 fl. oz.	120 mL
	1 cup	8 fl. oz.	240 mL
	1½ cups	12 fl. oz.	355 mL
	2 cups or 1 pint	16 fl. oz.	475 mL
	4 cups or 1 quart	32 fl. oz.	1 L
	1 gallon	128 fl. oz.	4 L
VOLUME EQUIVALENTS (DRY)	⅛ teaspoon	————	0.5 mL
	¼ teaspoon	————	1 mL
	½ teaspoon	————	2 mL
	¾ teaspoon	————	4 mL
	1 teaspoon	————	5 mL
	1 tablespoon	————	15 mL
	¼ cup	————	59 mL
	⅓ cup	————	79 mL
	½ cup	————	118 mL
	⅔ cup	————	156 mL
	¾ cup	————	177 mL
	1 cup	————	235 mL
	2 cups or 1 pint	————	475 mL
	3 cups	————	700 mL
	4 cups or 1 quart	————	1 L
	½ gallon	————	2 L
	1 gallon	————	4 L
WEIGHT EQUIVALENTS	½ ounce	————	15 g
	1 ounce	————	30 g
	2 ounces	————	60 g
	4 ounces	————	115 g
	8 ounces	————	225 g
	12 ounces	————	340 g
	16 ounces or 1 pound	————	455 g

	FAHRENHEIT (F)	CELSIUS (C) (APPROXIMATE)
OVEN TEMPERATURES	250°F	120°C
	300°F	150°C
	325°F	180°C
	375°F	190°C
	400°F	200°C
	425°F	220°C
	450°F	230°C

Resources

FAVORITE BOOKS

- **DAIRY-FREE GLUTEN-FREE BAKING COOKBOOK:** This is my first cookbook, filled with favorite baking recipes that are safe for anyone with celiac disease and a dairy intolerance. It is extremely educational on the various flours available and how to use them and has three recipes for the best gluten-free flour mixes to make at home.

- **GRAIN BRAIN:** *The Surprising Truth About Wheat, Carbs, and Sugar—Your Brain's Silent Killers,* by David Perlmutter, MD: This book shares the surprising and moving truth about what these foods do to break down the body. For some, it is hard to cut these foods out cold turkey, but it is important to try to avoid any white sugar or keep it as minimal as possible. This is a great book to open your eyes to understanding your body chemistry and the devastating effects of gluten.

WEBSITES AND ORGANIZATIONS

- **CELIAC DISEASE FOUNDATION.** Learn everything you need to know about this autoimmune disease and its effects. There are even ways to get involved to help others. celiac.org

- **AMY MYERS, MD.** "9 Signs You Have a Leaky Gut" If you have questions about what is going on in your body, and if you or someone you love is suffering from a food allergy, this will help guide you. amymyersmd.com/2019/02/9-signs-you-have-leaky-gut

- **BEYOND CELIAC.** This site will help expand your knowledge of celiac, how to live with it, and what foods you can eat. It is one of my favorite sites that I highly recommend. beyondceliac.org

- **U.S. FOOD & DRUG ADMINISTRATION, FOOD.** Learn about how the FDA regulates foods and their labeling so you and your family can stay safe. fda.gov/Food

- **DELIGHTFUL MOM HEALTH.** My trusted line of high-quality, natural health products that are safe and proven to get results. delightfulmom-health.com

- **NATIONAL CENTER FOR BIOTECHNOLOGY INFORMATION.** The National Center for Biotechnology Information advances science and health by providing access to biomedical and genomic information. ncbi .nlm.nih.gov

WHERE TO SHOP

- **THRIVEMARKET.COM.** A great choice to order high-quality natural foods and gluten-free products in the comfort of your home. They ship right to your door and their prices are affordable.

- **BUTCHERBOX.COM.** An all-natural, hormone-free organic meat delivery service. Their beef is organic, grass-fed, and grass-finished, and they have some of the best prices around. They also provide all-natural pork and bacon without nitrates and wild seafood. They deliver right to your door for free.

- **AMAZON.COM.** Find gluten-free flours and almost any ingredient you need. The prices are affordable and shipping is free with Amazon Prime.

- **SPECIALTY GROCERY STORES.** Some of the grocery chains that carry a lot of gluten-free flours and ingredients: Sprouts, Henry's, Whole Foods, Frontier Market, and Fresh Market. Shop their bulk section for most of the ingredients when possible to help save money on groceries.

Index

Acknowledgments

This book has been a gift of an opportunity for me to create it especially for you. It was hard to choose only 100 recipes because there are so many more that I wanted to share! On a daily basis we are surrounded by food, some healthy and some not so much. The recipes I chose to share here will help support a thriving body. I hope you make them year after year, relishing them over time with family and friends.

I want to acknowledge so many people who helped create this book with me and inspired these recipes:

To my publisher, Callisto Media, and my incredible editor, Daniel Petrino, and the rest of the hard-working team, including Anne Egan, who helped make this cookbook what it is today.

A huge thank-you to my husband, Kristopher, and our children, Chase and Curren! You guys are my rock and always show me love, support, and patience to allow me to continue adding new creations to the world.

To the ladies who are an influence in my life: my mother, Diane, and my grandmother, Nanny, who taught me how to cook from the first time I entered a kitchen. You two taught me the importance of family first, time together, and relishing a home-cooked meal with one another, slowly, even if it's a five-course dinner (my Italian side really taught me patience!). To my sister, Darlene, and sister-in-law, Tara, with whom I frequently chatted about upcoming recipe ideas and our favorite dishes. And to my amazing and wise mother-in-law, Jody, who suddenly passed away while I was writing this book. You are all my inspiration and are always there supporting and cheering me on and offering your wonderful advice.

And to God for making everything possible. I think Gandhi summed it up best with his famous quote: "Your beliefs become your thoughts, your thoughts become your words, your words become your actions, your actions become your habits, your habits become your values, your values become your destiny."

Last but not least, to you, my cookbook and blog readers: Thank you for your support, recipe suggestions, comments, emails, and more. They keep me excited about creating new recipes every single day! This is for you because you can do all things, even when you might not feel like you can. You can cook, you can bake, you can heal, and you can thrive! I hope these recipes give you the encouragement and the fuel you need to live your best life. And I hope you enjoy these recipes as much as I have enjoyed creating them for you!

About the Author

DANIELLE FAHRENKRUG is a healthy living, whole-food advocate dedicated to helping others regain and maintain their health and vibrance through healing, real food recipes. You can find her sharing recipes and tips on her popular blog delightfulmomfood.com. She specializes in creating simple and delicious gluten-free recipes the whole family will enjoy while educating readers on the benefits of the specific foods and ingredients in each recipe. You can also find her high-quality line of natural health supplements at delightfulmomhealth.com. You can follow her on Instagram, Facebook, and Pinterest (@delightfulmomfood). She lives in Buellton, California, with her husband and two boys.

9 781646 114986